LITERARY LANES *and* OTHER BYWAYS ✄ ✄
ROBERT CORTES HOLLIDAY

By ROBERT CORTES HOLLIDAY

In Collaboration with

ALEXANDER VAN RENSSELAER

LITERARY LANES
and OTHER BYWAYS

BY

ROBERT CORTES HOLLIDAY

NEW YORK
GEORGE H. DORAN COMPANY

I AM forcibly reminded of something.

During the years that I was employed in the publishing business I had a frequent experience. The author of a manuscript which he, or she, desired to submit for book publication would be determined to see me, as an editorial representative of the house with which I was connected, personally, face to face. The object of this author in this would be to warn me—not to read first, it might be, the first chapter of the manuscript, nor even perhaps, the second chapter.

I was by no means to do this, for by doing so I should obtain a totally false impression of the book. I should thereby be led completely astray as to its real interest and value. I'd be sure to be very much bored by, say, that first chapter; interest did not begin until, perhaps, page 114, where I was directed to commence reading. And then, it seemed, interest did not continue straight ahead. No, I was to skip several chapters specified, and then come back and pick up this part, in a peculiar order outlined by the author. In this way, and only in this way, would I, or presumably any reader, get the book right.

Now, of course, the obvious answer to such a complicated lot of instructions was this question. If that was the way the book ought to be read, why hadn't the author arranged the manuscript accordingly? And, suppose the book should be published, how on earth could the author expect the readers he hoped to acquire to know that in reading it they should proceed in so eccentric and confusing a fashion?

Thus this trepidation on the part of certain tender authors, generally authors, no doubt, of a first literary venture, would strike me as amusing, humorous. At the same time, I found it rather pathetic: at the root a nervous suspicion that there was something very much indeed wrong with the book, a haunting consciousness that it was very likely to be found gravely wanting—even, you felt, a fear of having the book read at all, lest it appear ridiculous, and the author a poor simp.

TO THE DREADFUL READER

Now I have just been reading the proofs of this book before you, this book of my own. And I find myself an author *very much in qualms*. Very much in qualms! For heaven's sake! let *me* tell *you, my* dreadful reader, personally, face to face, something about *this* book.

I implore you not to read this first chapter first. *Please, never* read this first chapter! It is thoroughly asinine. More, silly. It is an inconceivably shallow, sickeningly affected attempt, in a little-bright-eyes manner, to be cute. The human being, if you can call the creature that, who wrote the thing ought to be kicked in the seat.

The second chapter is not so absolutely puerile; there is, I think a grain of something not altogether detestable in it. The third chapter is unspeakable. Contemptible that piffling advantage has been taken in it of a diffident and first rate gentleman! The fourth chapter has an idea which might have been developed into something of fair interest to a reading person, if it had not been so scamped in method, and if the smirk had been throttled out of the style. The fifth chapter is intolerably dull, elephantine in its effort at playfulness, senile in its notion of humor. A few little things in it, borrowed from other sources, have a mild, a very mild quality of entertainment. The sixth chapter is pretty good. The style here, overjaunty of course, is carried off well enough. The wisp of a piece really says what it says a good deal better than you usually find the thing said. Skip the seventh chapter, anybody who may have nosed into the book thus far.

The eighth chapter is a not unamusing piece of journalism, quite industriously worked out. The ninth chapter is pretty sad, and the author's caddishness crops up every here and there, but the piece contains a small point or two. The tenth chapter may have its uses, in offering certain elementary suggestions in a matter which needs more attention of just this kind. The eleventh chapter is a reasonably able odd job of writing, and, perhaps, has some appreciable substance as a bit of social record. Likewise the twelfth chapter. The thirteenth chapter had a point which cries out to be made, but the loathsome bumptuousness of its manner I fear makes it merely absurd. The whole thing, this chapter, makes me squirm with embarrassment for the poor coxcomb who wrote it. The fourteenth chapter meant well but in its priggishness of tone is insufferable.

The fifteenth, the final chapter, is all in all an excellent performance. Here and there, particularly in the earlier part, the chapter is marred by deplorable lapses into flippancy of style, offensive antics of cheap smartness. But the matter presented is vigorous in its point of view, the writer obviously knows what he is talking about, he is thorough in his method, and by and large his manner reflects sincerity and earnestness. This, by the way, is the only article in this book which has not been printed elsewhere; several eminent editors have declined it.

Now why don't I rearrange the material in this volume as I would have it presented to the reader? Because the book has been put into type, it is no longer merely manuscript but many pounds of metal; wholesale shifting about of so much dead weight is not feasible in the printing business. By omission and revision why do I not try to improve the text—in the light of my awakened understanding? I *have* deleted and revised on the proofs as much as the printer will stand: and you can't make a silk purse out of a sow's ear. Why, then, don't I scrap the whole layout? The book was accepted by the publishers many months ago and for some time has been announced for forthcoming publication; the matter has in some considerable measure gone out of my hands. Also, as the various articles here reprinted were originally accepted for publication in journals and periodicals of wide circulation, were, indeed, solicited by the editors, I must assume that some people will like 'em.

But why did I ever stick the stuff together into a book at all? I might decline to answer that question on the ground that to do so would tend to incriminate me. However, having here put myself on the stand, I'll make a clean breast of everything, if I go to the chair for it. I had got into the habit of "pasting up" year after year journalistic articles of mine into very indifferent books, and, I suppose, like the bank embezzler already in deep, I thought that one more defalcation wouldn't matter.

If I am so much ashamed of this kind of thing why did I write it in the first place? As to that, as a lad I began well enough; I had my ideals; then, as time went by, I fell into the way of trying to imitate myself—with results less to the good. If it's of any interest to you to hear

[x]

it, I will say that I won't do this again; henceforth I will do my best to write right.

Permission to reprint the articles gathered into this volume has been courteously given by the editors of the following publications: *The Bookman, The Book Review, Advertising Fortnightly,* the *New York Herald.*

R. C. H.

New York, 1925.

CONTENTS

LITERARY LANES
AND OTHER BYWAYS

LITERARY LANES AND OTHER BYWAYS

I

WELL, I had quite a time of it. This was the way it went. I got shipped to San Francisco. And there I came upon one of the most colourful figures in our story of letters.

Out on the Pacific Coast what do the wild waves say? The wild waves—and all the people there—say, of literature, this—George Sterling.

Of course, I saw him. Jack London said it: "He looks like a Greek coin run over by a Roman chariot." He looks the poet—the poet that he is—the poet of old tradition. The poet of olden days, when a poet was popularly expected to be a picturesque figure, a Lord Byron, a Shelley, or something like that.

I read him out there. They all read him out there. Then I came back to New York. I said

[17]

all around about this and that about George
Sterling. And everybody replied: "Goodness
gracious me! Is he still going on? Why, I used
to admire him very much years ago. But I
thought he was dead, or something like that."

So the notion occurred to me that, by some
humble efforts even of my own, a kind of mis-
sionary work might be done. His books had for
some time been published by a very estimable
gentleman in San Francisco, his "cool grey city
of love," one Alec Robertson, a bookseller known
far and wide to the "trade." "Let's," I said to
myself, "get him published here in the East, too;
so that his light may shine again nation wide."

But was that as simple a matter to accom-
plish as you might think? It certainly was not,
I had to write him something like half a hundred
letters. He did not see any occasion for having his work "pushed." The artist went on his
quiet way—creating, after his fashion. When,
or if, the world found him, well and good. And
then, one of those aggressive publishers would
be likely to put a blurb on the jacket of
the book. And could he be trusted not to
say something immodestly eulogistic in an
advertisement?

[18]

However, we beat him down. We—the publishers with whom I was in cahoots—gave him our word of honour to tell the world that as a poet he was not so much. The matter of publishing his "Selected Poems" was arranged. Let the book but come out, I sighed with considerable relief—and the world find the artist! In this case, he should be a decidedly corrective influence to much tumult and gaudy shouting. His, we who are happy in knowing him know, is poetry in the "grand manner." He is a poet of the noble, rich and sounding line. No longer the fashion of the day. The excellent Walter Prichard Eaton not long ago wrote a little piece on "Contemporary Poetry and the Memorable Line." You can't, he contended, remember any of that written nowadays. We are too hurried here to argue anything. But we might throw out in passing an indisputable observation—beauty endures. Fashions do not.

Well, how did the thing come out? Why, when the book actually appeared Mr. Sterling suddenly became quite interested in its fortunes. He wrote, in a very beautiful hand, frequent letters to me and to his publishers. And, let us say, and so on. Let us hope that he is more

[19]

awakened now than he was before to the idea of going on actively with his career as a poet.

Now there are knocking about a number of people who are writers who are like George Sterling in this. They are artists whom the world has willingly let more or less go by. One of them is a young man of the name of Robert Nathan. This author has written, I understand, three or four books. One, a slender sheaf of verses called "Youth Grows Old"; one a novel (or something like that), slight in bulk, called "Autumn"; and one—the only volume of his which so far I have read—a story of some two hundred odd pages entitled "The Puppet Master." I see, from press opinions reprinted on the jacket of this volume, that far more thorough literary critics than I can claim to be, are pretty familiar with Mr. Nathan's work generally. Still, I take it, from my own meagre acquaintance with his talent, that he is far from being as well known as he should be.

It is difficult to tell precisely what the "The Puppet Master" is all about. It is difficult to tell precisely what that admirable recent book of short stories, "The Celestial Omnibus," is all about, or "Where the Blue Begins" is all about.

[20]

This much, offhand, may be said. There has been lately, when you look at the matter a moment, a most striking revival—or increase—of the kind of delicate, sure, fanciful, humorous, philosophical, pure literature which we used to find at rare intervals in such books as "The Little White Bird," "The Wind in the Willows," and "The Crock of Gold."

"The Puppet Master" is not, of course, quite like any of these, nor like any other book now going; but it is in spirit a notable return to things of that sort which spring from a delectable essence of spirit.

II

RUDOLPH VALENTINO, as he sailed for Europe not long ago, was quoted by the ship news reporters as saying that he received from 2,000 to 3,000 love letters a week. This is presumably the record in this matter. Though it might be interesting to know the relative correspondence of a like nature called forth by the gifts of the Prince of Wales, Mr. Jack Dempsey, Mr. John Barrymore and a number of others who are among the first in the hearts of admirers manifold. We do know that when anybody comes along with almost any kind of a deed or quality which arouses any degree of public attention his unsolicited correspondence considerably increases. This is an engaging light on the neighbourhood spirit of the world. A lady who is in the predicament of being tried for the murder of a gentleman friend is sure to be the recipient of a quantity of warming epistles by hands unknown to her. More or less recently, over in New Jersey a primitive farmerette, described in the papers as the "pig woman," who happened to be riding her mule by the scene close upon the time of a double murder, promptly received several proposals of marriage from ardent masculine souls not before within the circle of her acquaintance.

So it is natural enough that authors, too, should be favoured with many letters from without the bounds of their personal associations. Authors very popular indeed, doubtless, are thus very highly favoured. But those, too, who are authors only in a modest way receive their letters of spontaneous combustion origin. I have a friend who is an author of this kind, and the other day he was telling me something of his correspondence. To reply to something like 3,000 love letters a week—and to sustain an appropriate fervour—it strikes me would grow to be rather an arduous task. But my friend informs me that the matter of receiving and acknowledging a limited number of generous hearted missives coming from unexpected quarters is quite stimulating to one's sense of wellbeing. Well, I suppose this may very likely be.

He, my friend, had recently got a photograph. He said one came along every once in awhile. This one was about three feet in height. In a letter at hand referring to the picture, the subject of the portrait explained that in connection with a church fair in her town she would like to have it "named." The author was a bit puzzled, but he had concluded that the young lady meant for him to entitle it "Spring," or "Sappho," or something like that. The first prize for the name elected to be the best, she informed him, was to be a set of berry spoons. She desired him to keep the photograph. "But," he said, surveying its proportions, "where?" Among other presents suddenly sent my friend at various times by his readers he mentioned a home-made cake (somewhat crushed in transit) in which was (precariously) concealed a bottle of home-made wine, and a cylindrical carton quite six feet tall which when he unwound it (this was received at his club) proved to contain (to the high mirth of a group of his friends) branches of enormous length of pussywillow buds.

Another photograph which had come to him was a miniature snap-shot, which though full-face had been cut in half so that it revealed only one eye. The miss who wrote the note in which this was enclosed asked if he thought "anyone could be in love with someone they had never seen." She, it developed, was a "shut-in," whose only diversion was in reading; and my author friend felt her fragrant advances to be a very touching thing, which helped him, he said, to be a little "better." There was an old gentleman, too, who regularly sent him pressed weeds and grasses. And a "farmer's wife" (as she described herself) who gave a party, she subsequently reported, in which to read his first reply; and who turned out to be a very clever and stimulating literary correspondent. Also a group of children in a high-school who, their principal informed him, had chosen him as their "guardian," had written him. A number of firmly cemented friendships with persons of his own sex and age, my friend told me, had arisen from letters written him on the spur of the moment by strangers.

Endless, he found, was the number of young people who had the curiously fallacious notion that he could, by some mysterious turn of the hand, procure for them jobs in editorial offices. Very odd were some miscellaneous communications. One correspondent dwelt upon the number and shamefulness of the typographical errors in the author's latest book, and suggested that he send a list of them. But not, the letter later revealed, as a friendly service to be rendered gratuitously. Solicitous parents every now and then sought his advice as how best to prepare their sons or daughters for a writing career—the sons and daughters in some cases being in the neighbourhood of seven years of age.

III

A FELLOW doesn't know," remarked Royal Cortissoz one day, "what a quaint world it is until he paddles around in it a little." It seems that he had gone somewhere, at the invitation of a lady of the name of Smith, to make a speech—and he had found her to be the niece of an immortal German composer, or of an illustrious Russian novelist, or something like that.

Myself, I would sit at home and read the poems of Robert Frost, and articles about him that came along. Of several things there could be no doubt: he was the soul of New England; Puritan, as they make 'em, in tradition. "Stark" was the word one used concerning him. As one perspicacious critic has observed, winter lies over all his landscapes. And great is his "economy" of words. In humour how many of his most sympathetic readers find him meagre?

Then one day I paddled out into the world,

and I encountered Mr. Frost. He at once began to talk. He talked until lunch time, then we went to lunch. At three, or half past, the talk was unfinished, and it was his cordial idea that I come up and spend several days with him at his house in Vermont. He was, I understood, more or less of a farmer. So as midnight approached I supposed that it was time for me to let him get to bed. Nothing like that. For three nights running we sat up until the neighbourhood of four.

He is one of those persons one, who is not much good at talking to most people, finds to his surprise and vast comfort he can at ease talk with forever. And, one suspects, one of those men (the real talkers) who talk best in the company of one or two, when they ramble on and on, turning out the contents of their minds, as much as anything else to see for themselves what is there; but who before a larger audience are not at ease, often are inarticulate, frozen up. He talked, that was quite clear, not at all to sound clever, but in an amiable way groping—like a man with his hands out—toward his thought.

He talked, with much relish of that picaresque atmosphere, of his early days in San Francisco, the old "gun days," when his father was a news-

[28]

paperman who "burned himself out" at thirty-six. It was a customary prank when anybody threw a bottle from the beach for some of those along the shore to out and plunk at it. His father rather liked for him to run wild. He "saw a good deal for a little fellow, much more than he had seen back here." He left at twelve.

His father had "broken away"; he came back to New England, to play cribbage with his grandfather. Felt his grandfather didn't like him, didn't like his cap. He was "not consciously Bohemian," but Western, "not up to the mark." His fault, he should have gone to see his grandfather more. But the New England spirit altogether puzzled him, the economy, the repression. "There was nothing you could get against them to show how much they thought of you."

He made no money "that could be called money" until he was forty. Average earnings from his poetry for about twenty years ten dollars a year. His first real recognition, as we know, came to him from England while for a year or two he was residing there.

He talked of horse trading, likes that, trading. Of bee-keeping. Of characters who were "inarticulate poets," liked them because inarticulate, stuff *lived* rather than *written*. An appreciation of which he was immensely proud had come to him written on stationery bearing the letter-head of a hay and feed business, the writer saying that he had read one of Frost's poems over the rural telephone to his sister. He did not like to be long in the city, two or three days there tired him out. Also, living in the country he could keep out of literary "circles." He was "easy going," and in town might get "roped in." His wife was more severe, and could stave 'em off; though he could fight, too, perhaps at a pinch.

Every once in a great while he reads maybe half a dozen novels all in a bunch, to see if anything new in fiction has turned up. The way he knows how old he is, is by the number of those words which have passed through a popular vogue, about one a year—intrigue, register, complex, visibility. When his students ask him what they are to do in the time they owe to preparation for his classes he replies: "Spend those hours in not engaging in student activities and you'll have fulfilled the contract."

No, he couldn't undertake to write anybody letters; he "hated to write."

SMALL HOURS WITH R. FROST

We spoke of a prominent novelist who, with the rise of his fame, had got to be considerably "up stage." Frost shook his head. "That's my idea of *being good*," he said; "being a decent fellow, if you can." We discussed a little a poet whose work is very much in the "new" manner. "He fell into his stuff," said Frost, "by accident. He first tried to write the way he ought to write." Of the contemporary style of criticism, he remarked: "It is praise now to say all the things that used to be insults." Allusion was made to the expression of a very able and popular writer of fiction, that what he was trying to do in writing was, "to keep the ink out of it"; that is, as he meant it, to endeavour to present a transcript of life directly from the field, so to say, and not by way of the study. The phrase did not, upon some reflection, appear to Frost to be altogether satisfactory. "Not exactly to keep the ink out of it," he mused, "but to make the words your own—not something that has been used." By way of a little joke suddenly occurring to him he spoke with humorous disdain of books of synonyms and such things. The use of such volumes was like trying to "say it over." He happened to refer to the fact that the form he had very generally employed in his poetry had been iambic verse. And that his striving was for "speech rhythm."

IV

AN OUTLINE OF THE VAMP IN LITERATURE

I HAVE more or less recently become engaged in a new pursuit. It is one containing, I think you will readily admit, much colour. I have taken up collecting vamps. That is, in literature. Collecting vamps in real life, beyond doubt, would require qualifications to which I lay no claim.

But to form an intimate circle of vamps in literature, I have discovered, is an activity which furnishes one with abundant entertainment without any appreciable personal risk. And in contemporary fiction one finds the heyday of the vamp. I'd like to discuss this matter a little. Though I have, at the moment, space for no more than a very sketchy outline of this opulent subject. A really ambitious "Outline of the Vamp in Literature," by a hand more scholarly than mine, would be a work which should take its place among the most widely esteemed volumes of our day.

The vamp, of course, entered literature with the earliest records of mankind. For the matter of that, did not Eve vamp Adam? And there was Lilith before her. The pages of Homer are, so to put it, all cluttered up with vamps. Though there they are called sirens. The lusty Elizabethans were not behindhand in their portrayal of vamps. In one or another of her forms, the vamp flourished throughout the literature of the Restoration. Her trail is, indeed, through all literatures. It will supply very fair diversion for perhaps an hour or so if one will take a pencil and note down the names of the most celebrated vamps in literature that readily occur to him. One might make a start, say, with Madame Bovary.

But vamps have not been (outwardly, at any rate) the same in all ages. For instance, in much of the literature of the Victorian era, it may be remarked, the vamp appears in a disguise of protective coloration adapted to the current ideas and sentiments of the time. It was, indeed, when the "heroine" went out of fashion in fiction, that the vamp really came in as a leading lady, in her own character. At the present moment, if you are an up-to-date novelist, you cannot, of course, have a hero or a heroine, or an out-and-out villain, but you are certainly called upon by the most successful technique of the period to furnish a thorough-going vamp, solid mahogany all through, so to say.

The ingenuity of our novelists in their ambition to outdo one another in the creation of this character is a matter for wonderment. In "Cytherea," as an example, Mr. Hergesheimer came out with an arresting idea—the vamp, a most effective one, was a doll. Later, in "The Bright Shawl," he has again a symbol, but he lavishes all the resources of his full palette on the portrait of the supervamp, the Spanish dancer La Clavel.

In a number of the novels by the much advertised Younger Generation, practically all of the feminine characters are vamps, one not much more than any other. A remarkably human vamp, whose infant wears false curls, plays her part in Wallace Irwin's fine story, "Lew Tyler's Wives." She is a broad comedian. A rip-roaring vamp, whom it will be highly difficult for his competitors to surpass, is the one-time snake-charmer, later screen star, Zimbule, in Carl Van Vechten's book "The Blind Bow Boy."

[35]

She is designed to represent the zenith of unabashed young animal instincts. And she pretty nearly does.

In the first, and very striking story, "Little Emma," in "Picture Frames," by Thyra Samter Winslow, we have an excellent representation not of the gorgeous but of the demure type of vamp, one who plays very artfully the "little country girl." Mary S. Watts, in her recent, admirable novel of the Middle West, "Luther Nichols," presents a very subtle and aristocratic vamp in the person of one Miss Juliet Ordway, a highly cultivated young woman and only daughter in a family of much wealth. She vamps, by the way, the new family chauffeur, a young man with "smouldering eyes." The author's conclusion would seem to be that it was rather wrong for the young lady to do that. She should have stuck to her class.

Then there are current vamps in whom the element of vampishness is elusive. A memorable study of this type is given in the consummate little work of art which Willa Cather calls "The Lost Lady," a picture of pioneer railroad days in the West.

A vamp somewhat back in our chronology, but

one whom every now and then I recall with amusement, was the lady on "the train to New York" whom young Henry, in Samuel Merwin's "Temperamental Henry," took to be Lillian Russell.

The good Thackeray considered that he was presenting a good deal of an innovation when he issued "Vanity Fair," and announced it as "a novel without a hero." It would be a daring thing (but probably bad business) if a contemporary author should advertise his latest work of fiction as "a novel without a vamp."

V

BONS MOTS HERE AND THERE

"Do you not eat vegetables, Mr. Brummell?"

"Yes, madame, I once ate a pea," was the reply.

THERE is an excellent book, published some ten years ago, which every once in awhile I take down from my shelves, when I have nothing to do but to entertain myself. This volume is entitled "Dandies and Men of Letters," and the author is Leon H. Vincent. This title is not designed to imply, as when it was issued some of the reviewers of the book seemed to think was the case, that all of the figures who are the subject of the volume were *both* dandies and men of letters; but that some of the portraits are of dandies and others are of men of letters. Thus the volume, quite fittingly, opens with a very accomplished essay on "The Celebrated Mr. Brummell." Herein the author retrieves for us from various fading sources a bouquet of the *mots* of the illustrious Beau on which his reputation for great wit was founded. Their fragrance has not

[38]

withered away with time. I like especially the one about the pea.

That was a pleasant bit of drollery, too, when Brummell attributed a severe cold to the landlord's having put him into a room with "a damp stranger." Diverting, also, was his reply to a friend who asked him why he was limping: Brummell explained that he had hurt his leg, and the worst of it was "it was his favorite leg." And the neat comment of the Regency dandy would have served very appropriately for some of the weather of our present spring when an acquaintance asked him whether he had ever seen such an unseasonable summer. "Yes," replied the Beau, "last winter." This *mot*, as Mr. Vincent suggests, reminds one of Horace Walpole's "Spring has set in with its usual severity."

A man, a man with a light touch and no end of reading, could do far worse, had he the leisure, than to engage himself upon the composition of a thorough-going work on the subject of the *mot* throughout history, assembling some several thousand of them of different periods and countries. There is not in existence even a modest essay upon the subject; at least, if there is I have been unable to find trace of it. The standard works of general reference are very meagre here. They, some of them, give several illustrations of the definition of the term, such as: "Jeffrey. Contrib. Edin. Rev. (1844): 'Another *mot* of hers became an established canon at all the tables of Paris;' " but they supply no array of examples. A *mot* of the Athenians to Pompey the Great is referred to in one place, and in another Descartes is named as the author of the *mot,* "My theory of vortices is a philosophical romance"— not, I should say, an especially good one. The "Stanford Dictionary of Anglicised Words and Phrases" reminds us that it became absolutely the fashion, during the reign of terror, to make *bons mots* on the way to be guillotined; and from James Howell's "Letters" is cited the vogue in his day of keeping albums in which it was sought to have friends and approachable personages inscribe a sentiment known as "the *mot* of remembrance."

A *mot* is, in the precise meaning of the word, a *saying,* especially a brief saying, epigrammatic, pithy, forceful or witty; *bon mot,* literally, a good saying. And, I think we will agree, it should have the air of having sprung forth spontaneously; it should, at any rate, in effect, have

been a casual saying. The ancient epigrammat-
ical writers, Greek and Roman, were not, in
this view, authors of *mots*. Rochefoucauld in
his "Maxims," and Pope in his couplets, and
Franklin in his "Poor Richard," do not have
just the flavour we mean when we speak of a
mot. There are, of course, plenty of volumes
dealing with proverbs, adages, aphorisms,
epitaphs, anecdotes and set mottoes, but
they are little to the purpose when one is in the
mood for pungent sallies of the sort which we are
here discussing.

A sudden observation, a quick retort, may
have perfectly good title to the *distingué* name
of *mot* and not be at all a knock-down and drag-
out burst of humour. Stevenson, in his chapters
in "Memories and Portraits" on "Talk and
Talkers," thought it worth while to note this little pleasantry of a certain old-world gentleman,
Robert Hunter, Sheriff of Dumbarton, and
author of a law-book standard in its day: "We
were both Roberts; and as we took our places at
table, he addressed me with a twinkle: 'We are
just what you would call two bob.'"

Some time ago ("two bob" reminds me) I met
on the street an old friend, the late Robert Gil-

bert Walsh, for many years dramatic critic of
the New York *Evening Telegram*—and a descendant, by the way, of the family of Jane
Walsh, who married one Thomas Carlyle, a lady
reputed for nimbleness of mind. "How," I happened to remark by way of greeting, "how are
you getting on?"

"Only in years," was (with an airy gesture)
the reply. And that, a bit of less than nothing
as it is, we should not, I think, hesitate to call a
mot. It has the air, the *finesse,* which is the soul
of the peculiar thing which at the moment we
have in view. And there is there, too, a tiny barb
to the mind. . . . Who of us is not thus getting on——in years?

"It was a very little thing, but it was neat," is
by way of being the perfect appraisal of many
an excellent *mot.* That is Mr. Vincent's happy
comment upon one of the little handful of clever
and pointed sayings, of which record exists, of
Count Alfred D'Orsay. This particular *mot*
was apropos of a certain nobleman who, having
lost the use of his legs, was wont to wheel himself about in a Bath chair. Some one asked the
Count the name of the English peer. D'Orsay
replied, *"Père la Chaise."*

BONS MOTS HERE AND THERE

A pointed or vivacious utterance struck out on the spur of the moment, of course, loses much of its flavour when merely written down. Something of the aroma dies on the lips of the speaker. The look in the eye, the mobility of the features, the tone of the voice, an effect which cannot be recovered on the cold surface of a page, are often an essential part of the witticism. And, most of all, there is the electric spirit of the occasion. We have heard it said of this illustrious writer and of that one, by those who knew them, that their talk was far better than their writing. The *mot* is, by the very conditions of its nature, the most perishable of all works of art. Though it is a joy to hold to what we can of those which have tickled our fancy.

Everyone, doubtless, has lying about in his memory a very fair little collection of his favourite *mots*. No one, of course, will have forgotten Dr. Johnson's observation concerning the dog that walked on its hind legs; nor Lincoln's comment in regard to the proper length for a man's legs. Such classic sayings do not lose by long familiarity their power to amuse, nor their stimulating appeal to common sense. Every now and then one comes across an excellent *mot* which is all that is known of the obscure person who made it. One such is recorded (by a commentator upon Swift) of "a widow lady of very respectable family," Mrs. Seneca, of Drogheda, who kept an inn where the great Dean slept one night. In the morning Swift made a violent complaint of the sheets being dirty.

"Dirty, indeed!" exclaimed Mrs. Seneca; "you are the last man, doctor, that should complain of dirty sheets."

Yes, he had just published the "Lady's Dressing-room," a very dirty sheet, indeed.

It is pleasant to be surprised by an amiable *mot* where little expected. Boswell one time asked Dr. Johnson why Pope said some lines which he repeated. "Sir," said the Doctor, "he hoped he would vex somebody." But, after all, Pope appears to have died bravely and cheerfully enough. His doctor, so the story goes, was offering him one day the usual encouragements, telling him his breath was easier, and so on, when a friend entered, to whom the poet exclaimed, "Here I am, dying of a hundred good symptoms." This suggests, of course, another deathbed *mot,* the famous, "I am afraid, gentlemen,

I am an unconscionable time a-dying," of Charles Second.

As there are authors who live in fame by a single poem, so there are great personages who have, so far as the records go, been inspired but once to a witty saying. Queen Victoria is not reputed to have been much given to epigrammatic utterance. But that was a nicely turned phrase when she remarked that Gladstone spoke to her as if she "were a public meeting."

And sometimes the sayings of a man who has acquired a great reputation as a wit do not, upon our returning to them, hold up. I happened to mention to a young librarian the other day the sort of thing I was in the mind to regale myself with. He at once suggested Oscar Wilde. Now and then, indeed, Wilde said some very fair things. That was not without merit, his remark to the effect that the fundamental human passion, our love of self, is "a life-long romance." But I think today you would find most of Oscar's obviously cooked-up epigrams and aphorisms lamentably flat. They have lost their edge. Indeed, one is now inclined to feel, they were little more than "flip" to begin with. All his real ideas, his ideas of art, I suspect, he got from

Whistler, anyhow. We have Jimmie's *mot* upon this: "I wish I had said that!" Wilde exclaimed of something the Master had just said. "You will, Oscar; you will," was Whistler's reply. *That*, undeniably, has plenty of sparkle. So great in his heyday was Mr. Whistler's reputation as a wit that, we recall, it was said anyone could produce mirth in a cultivated company by merely prefacing a remark by the phrase "as Whistler once said;" and, further, it was declared that anything good that anyone happened to say was sure to turn up later as something "Whistler once said." It has been argued, too, that the barbed *mots* of the author of "The Gentle Art of Making Enemies" and "The Baronet and the Butterfly" were wofully unworthy of the painter of "The Mother," "Miss Alexander," and some half a hundred other masterpieces. It puzzled George Moore (until he found an ingenious theory of explanation) that the man who was capable of spending the afternoon painting like one of the greatest could then rush off to polish the tail of an epigram "possibly good enough for *Punch*."

Well, that was his way. A *mot* is not made to stand for a man as a monument. One may,

I think, still find a round number of Whistler's
very good. There was witty perspicacity in his
reply when a person asked him who "may be"
the greatest black and white artist in the England of the time, and he answered "Phil May."
It was an apposite fling at "gush" when, to the
lady who purred to him that there was no one
like Whistler and Velasquez, he retorted: "Ma-
dam, why drag in Velasquez?" He expressed
the fundamental principle of all good art in the
deft: "Nature is always wrong." And, certainly,
he put into a nutshell the whole ardour of creation
in his splendid phrase, "an artist's career always
begins to-morrow." That recalls to my mind a
fine saying of another American painter, Edward Simmons, which I have often heard him
use (it is not, I believe, in his book, "From Seven
to Seventy"): "Each new morning is a virgin.
So up with all one's spirit and woo her!"

Perhaps the most famous, the one which has
been most widely relished, of our home-grown
American *mots* was Mark Twain's comment on
mistaken newspaper reports of his death, that
they were "greatly exaggerated." A Mark
Twain witticism which has had little currency
was told to me one time in Los Angeles, by a

gentleman of the name of Thomas Miranda, who is connected with the motion picture business there. Mark, visiting relatives of Mr. Miranda, left his cigar ash all over the house—on the mantel, piano top, window sills. This was carefully gathered into a fruit-jar by reverent members of the family, and he was asked to autograph the label pasted onto the jar. He wrote: "These are positively my ashes.—S. L. Clemens."

We are inclined, I suspect, to think of the *bon mot* as something we read of, something which came about much more naturally in the social intercourse of other times and lands than our own. We quite expect to stick in our thumbs and pull out such plums from books of memoirs of yesterday, as well as of long ago. In "Myself Not Least," the reminiscences of one "X," a chatty volume published not long ago, and which I was reading the other day, the author relates that one of the best of the stories told by Charles Brookfield was an account of his finding Sir Charles Wyndham seated in Garrick's chair at the Garrick Club at the time he was acting in "David Garrick."

"My dear Wyndham," Brookfield cried, with

more than his usual heartiness, "I must say you look more and more like Garrick every day."

This delighted Wyndham, who purred vehemently until Brookfield added, "And less and less like him every night."

Another of his favourite stories (given in the same volume) was that of his remark to "old George Grossmith," "My dear George, I never realised what a gentleman you were until I met your brother Weedon."

Doubtless, the cultivation of polished wit in conversation is not a pastime very general among us. But there are still with us makers of *bons mots par excellence.* The first of these today, I should say, is Oliver Herford. He has the flavour of olden pages.

One time (I do not know whether or not this little story has before found its way into print) a distinguished guest was being shown about the clubhouse of The Players. The party paused before a death-mask of the author of "The Rivals." The visitor looked somewhat startled. "And so that," he exclaimed, "is the death-mask of Richard Brinsley Sheridan! Why, how emaciated he looks! I had always thought of him as a gay, rollicking, jovial blade."

"Well," observed Mr. Herford, "you know he wasn't feeling very well when that was taken."

Another time, a friend, a writer of some little parts, remarked to Mr. Herford: "Ah! But you're a genius."

Oliver wheeled upon him with the retort: "You're another!"

Herford sayings could be collected from the memory of his friends to fill a fairly sizable chapter. One more must here suffice. Said Mr. Herford to the æsthetic gentleman: "Why do you call yourself a 'photograph*ist*,' why not a photographer?"

The reply was: "Don't you call yourself an artist?"

"No," answered Mr. Herford; "I'm an ar*ter*."

A very entertaining incident in journalism which may appropriately be recorded here was pleasantly rounded out by a touch from Don Marquis. The story goes to the tune of "With an Urn on the Table and a Good Song Going Round." The prize typographical error of our time appeared in one of the leading American literary magazines sometime during the course of the world war—in fact, the magazine was *The Bookman,* though this was before the editorship of Mr. Farrar. The writer of an article had referred to Keats' "Ode on a Grecian Urn." The printer, with his mind filled with the news of the day, set the title to read, "Ode on a German Urn." Mr. Marquis, on being told of the joke, murmured meditatively, "Grecian stein."

Kelly pool apparently is a social activity highly stimulating to the production of *mots*. Ray Irvin, magazine artist, playing the other day, amiably remarked of an opponent in the game (a rather headstrong player, if that is not too intrusive an aside): "He holds the secret of that shot in the hollow of his head."

Again, A. E. Thomas, American playwright, at the same table recently observed that: "It takes a major operation to extract money from a minor poet."

On another day when Mr. Thomas was in the game an onlooker remarked to another player who was striving to say bright things: "Be careful of your lines. Al Thomas will use them in his new play."

"Well," put in Royal Cortissoz, art critic, of the *New York Herald-Tribune,* "don't you want to be a fly embalmed in amber?"

Pool players, it would seem, have a gift for

lively speech anywhere. A friend one day ran into John Wolcott Adams (celebrated both as an illustrator and a pool player) on West Twenty-second Street. "What are you doing around this neighbourhood?" asked the friend.

"I live here," answered Mr. Adams.

"Why, I used to live on this block," said the friend. "Before it ran down," he added.

"Well, they've got the very same cops here now," remarked Mr. Adams, "so you'd better hurry along."

Baltimore has a bookseller of a very pretty wit. His name is Thomas Janvier, and as this paragraph will show, he considers it desirable to be born at an early age. His casual letters usually are several pages in length, typed single space, and with a quirk in nearly every line. He quaintly carried his merriment into even his catalogues. In one of his lists of first editions, rare books and old prints he follows the title and description of a book, published in 1874 and announced to be in his stock, with this comment: "First edition. A good copy. Very scarce. A book dear to all fortunate enough to have been born in the seventies or eighties. *Personally I wish I had been born in the thirties or even tens or twenties.*"

BONS MOTS HERE AND THERE

It is an admirable thing to hold one's own in this world. Richard Malchien, actor, erstwhile illustrious fencer, one time talking playfully with a group of friends declared: "No, he was not going to 'give his corpse' to Westminster Abbey." "Quite right, Dick!" exclaimed Jules Guerin, painter; "you hang on to it." No autobiography extant, by the way, has so magnificent a title as the one which Mr. Malchien has, in jovial fancy, hit upon for his own. It is "Pearls Before Swine." The title is as far as he has got.

But the best of all Mr. Malchien's sayings, and a line meet to be graven upon the enduring tablets of humour, came about in this way. He happened to remark to a friend that he was fifty-seven years of age. "Are you, indeed!" commented his companion; "why, you hardly look that." "Oh, my goodness," Richard declared, as he had abused his constitution. "Why!" he exclaimed, "if I'd taken any care of myself at all I might have been ninety right now." A curious commentary on good habits as a short cut to old age.

Charles Hanson Towne is authority for a striking illustration of the dangers attendant upon

growing better and better day by day. Lola
Fisher, stage star (he tells), said that she had
tried the Coué method, but being impelled to
knock wood so much she bruised her finger so
badly that she had to see a doctor about it.

A pleasantry presenting a happy case of af-
fluence in poverty is related now and then by
Richard Le Gallienne. A writer of the name of
Sadakichi Hartmann flourished in New York
a number of years ago. His work was directed
to an audience of the elect; at any rate, it was
not of a kind which sells widely. But, he was
fond of saying, "he did not care how poor he was
so long as he lived in luxury."

In inscribing a copy of his book an author
every now and then turns up a pleasant conceit.
With the object of stirring him up a bit, a friend
of Christopher Morley told him, when that book
was quite new, that he had heard that "Where
the Blue Begins" was a dog story. Mr. Morley
sent his friend a copy of the book with this commentary following the inscription: "N. B. This
is a 'dog story' in the same sense that 'The
Hound of Heaven' is one."

The staid pages of history are happily punc-
tuated ever and anon with a *mot*. Researches

into that rich and vast field are beyond the compass of this little essay, but I may as well put down an item that my eye happened to light upon just yesterday. Of Thomas Wharton it is recalled that, referring to his Peace of Utrecht, he observed that it was like the Peace of God—it passed all understanding.

And, of course, from the storehouse of the world's fiction a bedroom shelf of volumes could be compiled devoted to the sapient utterances and brilliant flings of characters not prone to mortal death. But should we wander there in our discussion of this theme we'd be never done. However, I cannot stay my hand from noting a saying which suddenly crosses my mind at the moment, and which I have always reckoned a very spirited one. It is that of Mr. St. Ives, you will remember, when he declared: "When I can't please a woman hang me in my cravat."

Now we have just time remaining to us here to turn to an entertaining kind of kink in talk which for our purpose we may call Malaprop *mots,* though it may be that you prefer to call them "bulls." Things like this: A young man connected in an aristocratic way with the publishing business the other day asked, very seri-

[55]

ously, a friend of his: "Can you keep a secret— even" (as a cautious after-thought) "in your cups?"

"But you know," said the other, "I don't drink now."

"Then, maybe," said the young man, hesitatingly, "I'd better not tell you."

A second: An actor before mentioned in these pages announced to one sitting beside him in the billiard-room that he had written a letter to a friend of theirs. "What did you tell him?" asked the other.

"I don't know," the correspondent blankly replied; "I just put it in the mail-box."

And a third, an instance of sex not yet conferred. "Boy or girl?" a well-known editor's wife asked her husband, concerning the newly born child of a couple of their acquaintance.

"I don't know," he replied, trying to think hard; "guess they haven't named it yet."

A number of other lightsome sayings of this *genre* begin to recur to me. Alanson Hartpence, old-time friend of Alfred Kreymborg, one time alluded to a complicated matter to figure. It was the instance of an acquaintance of his who sometimes referred to "the first time I first quit drinking."

I recall, too, an account of what might be called an impersonal birth. A friend of mine who had just returned from a trip through the South was telling me of an elderly coloured gentleman whom he had met down in Kentucky, and whom he happened to ask if he had been born in that neighbourhood. "Well, no; personally," was the reply—"personally, I wasn't born here. But I might jes' as well have been; I was born jes' across the line."

Then there was the case in the papers, I remember, of the immorally virtuous young woman. The affair was one of marital trouble between a couple moving in rather gay circles. The wife nonplused the court by asserting that several years before, her married life had "morally ceased." And she stuck to it, in exactly those words. Maybe her lawyers had instructed her to say "virtually ended."

Indignation is sometimes possibly the occasion of a charmingly Malaprop *mot*. A young woman of my acquaintance was much incensed at the way a recent New York election had gone. "All of those old people just voted that way," she exclaimed, "because they thought they would get back light beer and wine!" Dark beer (alas, for the wets!) even then to remain taboo.

Surprise, suddenly confusing the faculties, is often-times another source of comical exclamations. I remember one day when a young woman who evidently had entertained a false idea of the temperature abruptly came upon a sheeted pond, and exclaimed: "Why, is that ice frozen!" And record should be made of the Malaprop *mot* of a young woman writer lately turned housewife, who asked the butcher for "a shoulder of tongue."

The unconsciously mirth provoking sayings of children, of course, are never ending. One which has remained in my mind as a striking piece of historical criticism was this. Mrs. Joyce Kilmer was one time telling a young son of hers about the rise of the Dutch Republic. "But," the boy wanted to know, "how could the Dutch whip the Spanish, when they are such fighters, and the Dutch are so slow?"

His mother explained how the Dutch opened the dykes and flooded the land. The boy considered this stratagem a moment, and then remarked: "Clever but lazy." A remarkable example of indolence overcoming savagery.

And sometimes a little child will lead an elder into a bright saying. Mary Roberts Rinehart has a granddaughter named after her. In the no distant past, when the child was a very few years old, and was being wheeled one day in the park a passerby, pausing to admire her, pleas antly inquired: "And what is your name?"

"Mary Roberts Rinehart," piped up the child.

"Goodness me!" exclaimed the astonished questioner; "you don't say so! Why, I read a book of yours just the other day."

Then there are the *Awful Efforts*. Their commonest form is that of a pun. Myself, I have been a great sufferer from such sallies—because of my name, the connotation thereof. Anyone, I doubt not, who happens to have a name which invites a play of cheerful spirits endures a sad lot. Now you might suppose that anybody would suspect that I had heard the joke before: "Holliday. . . . holiday. . . . Christmas. . . . New Years. . . . You have a holiday all the time, I see. . . . Ha! ha!" But no. These many years have I seen the faces of those I meet light up as though with a novel idea when they hear my ill-advised name, and been called upon to join in the gaiety provoked by it, at an introduction, in the minds of endless new acquaintances. Ha! ha! That's good, all right! Well, one should not be a bear, and there are worse things in the world, no doubt, than continually being happily accepted as a target for innocent jollity.

An exceptionally awful effort in this direction, I think, was the mercurial comment of E. V. Lucas upon his making the acquaintance of the lady famous as Marcella Burns, head of the book department of Marshall Field and Company. He said (he actually did): "I shall always think of her as Booksella Burns."

Harry Kemp was around not long ago with some particularly sad ones. He had just returned from abroad, and he related how upon setting out he had announced that he was "going to Paris to be a parasite, and to Budapest to be a pest." He rounded out his dreadnought joke by reporting that someone remarked, "Why go?"

One more of this species should be enough. A writer whose name is fairly well known (but which from courtesy to him is here withheld) went one day into a prominent New York bookshop for a chat with an accomplished bibliophile engaged there. A set of a new edition of Casanova had just come into the shop. The bookseller was eager to have this handsome affair shown to his friend. After looking over the volumes the visitor thanked the other for his attention to him, and in parting said: "I'm glad to have ob-scene that."

Mention has been made of the little volumes available presenting collections of epitaphs. They, epitaphs, seldom have the natural turn of a spontaneous expression. But there is one I recall which, it seems to me, has a very fresh and fragrant quality. It came from the hand of Thomas Nelson Page, who wrote for the stone to his young wife: "Here lies all that is mortal of an angel;" and is quoted in the memoir of the Virginia novelist by his brother, Rosewell Page.

VI

THE ADVERTISING WAGON AND THE STAR

EVERY once in awhile since time began somebody has set out to start something. A religion, perhaps, or a revolution, or something like that.

Now persons who have given particular notice to such matters have observed that to carry on anything several things are required. A well built organization, it has always appeared, is a useful thing to have in hand. And a good cause, it seems, has in the long run much the better betting chance over a bad one. That is, if you really haven't anything worthwhile to sell you're going to get found out in the end, and will have to shut up shop, whether you're a poet or a Presidential candidate.

But one of the prime things for success in carrying on, it is quite evident, is some kind of a symbol—a cross, a flag, the mark of Aldus the printer, the celebrated "white lock" of Jimmie

Whistler, Roosevelt's "big stick," the elephant of the American Republican party. People, the way they are made, have to have something to tie to. Otherwise, they are more than likely to forget today that yesterday you set out to start something. A man can get interested in something which becomes familiar to him. He recognises a repetition of the same picture as an acquaintance. He loves, when it appeals to him, a familiar figure. It was not for nothing that Napoleon always appeared in a shabby overcoat and on a meagre white horse (amid resplendent officers), nor that Charlie Chaplin's affecting moustache and shoes remain the same.

They created what scientific advertising men today have come to call "an established atmosphere and layout style" for the purpose of "visual influence." And anybody will admit that they have not been so bad in "sustaining reader interest." They, each in his way, put up right off a "central thought"; and, being no slouches in the way of persistence, they held on toward a magnificent "cumulative effect." In short, they "trademarked their advertisements."

We say, for instance, "Napoleonic," and we say "to kodak"—same sort of thing: the words

by dint of continual knocking about have been
caught in the woof of the language. Little drops
of water, little grains of sand, make the mighty
ocean, and so on. Hammer, hammer, hammer.
Individuality. Distinctive character. And the
rest of it. Great geniuses in advertising instinc-
tively knew the ropes long, long before the advent of the advertising profession. As ever in
any art, what is as fresh as the morning is as
old as the eternal hills.

The lesson today is this: You (or I) may
have started something. Our tastes may run to
business, and perhaps we have set up a store, or
are engaged in the manufacture of a certain
product. We know we've got something good,
and we naturally want to tell people about it.
Now if we tell something about ourselves to a
person who is busy about something else (as most
people are) he probably won't hear a bit of what
we say. We have to keep on telling him. Then
after awhile he'll begin to think that maybe something is being said to him. And he'll look up.
The remarkable point about this is that when he
looks up he will remember to have heard what
we have been saying to him all the while.

Learned university professors talk forever and

a day about something which they call Psychology. Learned advertising men have written copiously about a thing which they call "continuity" in advertising. There is no need, however, for simple natures like ourselves being thus grand, gloomy and peculiar. We merely want to be widely known, and long remembered.

In the little matter, therefore, of our producing a permanent impression on the popular mind we're not such dumbbells as not to know that talking about ourselves in a haphazard way won't get us much forrarder. The advertiser whose advertisements are not in some way trademarked sails a rudderless course. A brilliantly coined name like "Uneeda," or the perpetual use of an actual name like "Ford," has ofttimes gone a long way in winning—and holding—public attention. A hypothetical Eskimo, or Don-Marquisian Aunt Jemima, frequently serves mighty well in keeping the audience from walking out on the show. A striking slogan such as "A Skin You Love to Touch," or "Built Like a Skyscraper," has been made to bring home a good deal of bacon. And a fundamental appeal aimed at some universal weakness of the flesh, such as susceptibility to *fear, pride, embarrass-*

ment, desire for success and so on, *continuously applied,* has done much in piercing through.

Again, there is much more to the springs of successful life than just signs and symbols. There is subtlety. Without the aid of any mystic emblem, like (let's say) the old-time cigar-store Indian, the cumulative value of continuity in the physical appearance of advertising—as they say, the "format"—it is quite observable makes an effective call to human nature. The consistent use of a typographic or illustrative style (as employed, for one example, in the LaFayette layouts) is a flash in advertising which says, "Here's another message from so-and-so."

This "family resemblance" throughout one's public appearances has been fairly well proved by many veteran advertisers—from Adam on down to Messrs. Hart, Schaffner & Marx—to have just as great a value as the patent trademark. "Tickle your type and make it talk," is a dictum of a great typographer. A style of type-face, or the repetition, maybe, of a distinctive border, may be made in time to tell instantly of the great name-blown-in-the-bottle brand.

Further, there is the *manner* of saying. Tiffany never says anything but "Diamonds,

Pearls." To say more would be to detract from that consummate smartness of effect. In fact, it would probably be ruinous. The casual reader of the papers spots Lord & Taylor as readily as he would Doug and Mary.

Continuity may be retained by an advertiser through years of campaigning, without sacrifice of variety. Witness: Campbell soups, Yale locks, Mazda lamps, Camel. Other examples, various. The device is a durable *idea*. In the case of Mazda, for instance, the theme of, so to say, the Greek chorus is Light.

Men have risen to great power by riding day in and day out just a few simple ideas. Mr. Coolidge is such a man. He is not "full of ideas," as the popular expression puts it; but he *is* full of his ideas. In his speeches the same thoughts recur perpetually. He finds them applicable to any problem. And they are *Coolidge*.

Let it be remembered, too, that often the advertiser is likely to tire of his make-up long before the public does—he sees it much more. Maybe Napoleon sometimes yearned to give his old clothes to the poor. And one has frequently heard of celebrated actors and novelists who grew weary, at times, of themselves as *the world loved them.*

In a word—let us, who would make ourselves *memorable,* hitch our wagon to an idea, and follow that idea as it were a star.

VII

IT is time to view with alarm the rising tide of
humour everywhere about today. This men-
ace to the solemnity of life is rapidly passing out
of all bounds. Turn whatever way you will and
you will find appalling evidence of the humour
which has become one of the phenomena of our
time and nothing less than a monstrosity.

Take advertising. There are men now living
and not beyond their prime who can readily recall the time when any man who had a product
to sell regarded the advertising of it as a serious
matter. This was business, a sacred thing; and
the mere suggestion of an element of jocularity
entering into the affair would have been viewed
with horror. Now what? Why, one example,
by reason of its glaring nature, should suffice.
John Held, an out-and-out humourist, is repeatedly employed to make drawings for advertisements.

Take journalism. Concerning the hold upon our people of, for instance, the comic strip what is one to say? But take those aspects of journalism which were once august. Take—just take it!—the editorial page. A book, a noble book, called "The Spirit of the Public Journals; or, the Beauties of American Newspapers, for 1805," a collection from "nearly one hundred vehicles of information" published in 1806, shows what the editorial once was. In this volume are gathered editorials or articles on "The Seasons," "Winter," "Return of Spring," "Autumnal Reflections," "Affections," "Love," "Hope," "Truth," "Modesty," "Deceit," "The Idler," "Begin in Time," "Fashion," "The Grave." Not a particle of humour in any of those ideas. Today you have no assurance that you will not find on the editorial page of any one of the country's leading newspapers a light touch and a humorous fancy. Think of it!

Or take literature. Good heavens, take that! What was the outstanding purpose apparent in the "Garlands," the "Miscellanies," the "Repositories," and so on so much current in the days of our grandfathers? Solemn instruction. Moral improvement. The inculcation of refined manners. Inspiration toward the need for spiritual salvation. Particularly, and most wisely, for the young, and in especial for the young of the feminine sex. Edmund Lester Pearson, in his volume "Books in Black or Red," has an excellent chapter on the books devoted to uplifting the youthful female character during the 1830's and 1840's.

Is there any need for one to ask what the situation in this respect is now? Do we not know, for one thing, that one of the most successful books of recent seasons was a volume in which instruction in polite conduct, in *etiquette,* was mocked? Would a parent today feel that his child would have any care for a little volume of "Moral Emblems?" No, he would probably procure for his child a copy of Carl Sandburg's "Rootabaga Pigeons," and very likely find relish in it himself—a book in which humour reigns unrestrained. Or, like as not, Mr. Van Loon's apocalyptical piece of delirium, "Wilbur, the Hat," dizzy all parts through, and well calculated to put anybody sufficiently out of his head for the moment to see things straighter than usual.

Our most important contemporary works of fiction, the exalted productions of our most distinguished literary artists, are parodied and flouted in such a piece of unalloyed humour as "The Triumph of the Nut," by Christopher Ward. One would think, to use Omar's word, that we had living humourists enow. But, apparently, at present the taste for humour is insatiable. Fragmentary pieces of humour by Mark Twain are unearthed and issued in new volumes.

"Annuals" of humour are got up. Humour on top of humour—humour comes to us from over the seas. Two new volumes composed of contributions to the pages of *Punch* pass beneath my eye. Can it be possible that in trouble-worn foreign lands humour flaunts itself now as it does here? Alas! it may not be wholly untrue. The English translator of a new edition of a long-persisting work of humour, called "Master Tyll Owlglass," states that much of the success of an earlier edition of the book must unquestionably be assigned to "the increasing sense of humour which is to be found in England." And *two* different versions in English of this "Gil Blas" of German mediæval story have appeared fairly recently.

Surely, if we would preserve to ourselves one

atom of our age-old heritage of solemnity, it is, as the chap said, time to call a halt to this infectious onslaught of humour.

And another formidable and insidious matter, closely allied to the grip obtained on us by humour. That is the fearsome currency of the essay. This marks a crumbling of the precious possession of tradition. No fact is better known to the publishing business than that just a few years ago it was considered economic madness, at any rate professional heresy, not to regard books of essays as what the book trade terms "plugs," and a drug on the market. An ironbound tradition had become erected in the publishing world, at least in the United States, to the effect that, except in very exceptional cases, books of essays were impossible as a publishing venture.

Then in some idiosyncratic moment a manuscript volume or two of essays was accepted for publication—and the harm was done. Volumes of essays began to go. The thing, getting up little volumes of essays, spread like wildfire. Last Christmas season there were so many books of essays, by such a host of essayists, that it did not seem that any one of the books could sell more than a few copies, if trade in the books was to be at all distributed over the lot of them. Practically all of them sold pretty well, some very well. Thus we see that last year the total consumption of essays in the United States was a serious thing. And the essay-taking habit among our people seems to be on the increase. There are probably more volumes of essays put up for sale this year than last. There are essays now calculated to lure into their toils nearly every type of mind. Where will this matter stop?

The situation, it must now be clear to anyone, calls for decisive action on the part of the citizens of the Republic who are not already too far gone in humour and essays for sober thought. And this brief survey of certain tendencies at work today on the minds and character of our people cannot begin to tell the whole truth.

VIII

SHIFT, SMOCK, CHEMISE OR NIGHTGOWN

YOUR nightgown should be fifty-two inches long. And fifty-eight inches around. It should have a hem of two inches. The minimum length of a nightgown now is fifty inches. With other minimum measurements in proportion. If you are not yourself fifty-two inches long, why, of course, you can take your nightgown up. And if you are ever so long indeed you've got a margin to let out. Suit the requirements of your own personality, of course, as to decorative effect. There is no edict from those who hold sway over the length and breadth of nightgowns as to that. The official figures here communicated to the nightgown wearing public relate to the garment as it comes from the store.

Formerly you didn't know how long a nightgown was. Nobody did. Nightgown-wearers used frequently to be under the necessity of holding nightgowns up to them in the aisles of department stores. This, some felt, was awkward. And often when a nightgown was got home it didn't gee at all with one's other nightgowns. One's nightgown wardrobe was inclined to be motley. And then there was the matter of price. When a nightgown-wearer found that a decidedly skimpy nightgown had nicked her more than a very ample *robe-de-chambre* she very naturally was apt to feel that she had been gypped.

This demoralised condition of affairs in the matter of nightgowns has existed since the world began. That is, ever since nightgowns, of any sort, came in. Eve's nightgown, presumably, was her day gown, too. And the simple system of dress of having one article of apparel for both sleeping and waking, it would seem, prevailed for some considerable time afterward. The subject of nightgowns is pretty much wrapt in darkness, historically. Some savant would find a very pretty subject to his hand in a history of the nightgown. Or, if he would be more ambitious still, why not a history of feminine underwear. It's a very engaging idea, I think. And I'm sure the author, if gifted with a pleasant style, would readily find a publisher. Learned men who are librarians shake their heads sadly when you ask them about *lingerie*. They send you to the room devoted to art and architecture.

CHEMISE OR NIGHTGOWN

There you find that the nightgown is a very shy thing. Volumes on costume give the eager student a very diffident view of nightgowns.

From the plates he would judge that the ancient Greek statues slept in a sort of winding-sheet carelessly disposed. Anyhow, the night garments (if such they be) of the lady statues are presented as long. In what did burning Sappho sleep? Cleopatra? Lady Flora. . . . Hipparchia. . . . Thais. . . . Heloise. . . . Dante's Beatrice? What fashion draped in sleep the fair white feet of Nicolette? Maiden and Queen, no man may say.

Our heritage of literature throws but little light on nightgowns. In "Macbeth" is the line, "Get on your nightgown, lest occasion call us." In the "Book of Curtasye" (1400) we find, "bryngis he forthe nyght-gown also." In Smollett's "Gil Blas," "She put on a thin night-gown which lay at the bed's feet." There's something —*thin*. Some recent styles have sought ultra transparency. John Evelyn, of the time of Charles II, speaks thus of a lady's wardrobe:

> Twice twelve smocks of Holland fine,
> With cambric sleeves rich points to joyn,
> Twelve more for night, all Flanders laced,
> Or else she'll think herself disgraced.

But there is no clue as to the length. One would expect something definite from Pepys. He merely says at one place: "Somewhat vexed at my wife's neglect in leaving of her scarfe, waist-coat and nightdressings in the coach to-day that brought us from Westminster though I confess she did give them to me to look after." In "Nicholas Nickleby" on more than one occasion "Mrs. Squeers came in still habited in the familiar night jacket." *Blackwood's Magazine,* in 1828, spoke of "the Hebrew women who. . . had been accustomed to wear no night chemises at all." And there you are. There may be in the storehouse of the world's literature a bit more than this about nightgowns but I can't at the moment put my finger on it.

Dick Steele in the *Tatler* remarked of someone that "she carried off the following goods—eight night-shifts." Again, Pepys relates this: "About the middle of the night I was very ill—I think with eating and drinking too much—and so I was forced to call the mayde who pleased my wife and I in her running up and down so innocently in her smock." Shift. . . smock. . . chemise. . . you will have noticed that all of these names have been in use as terms for what we are accustomed to call the nightgown. Yes, although we think of a smock now as an affair worn (especially by English rustics and later adopted by artists) over other clothes—like overalls, the dictionaries confirm the fact that a shift was a smock and a smock was worn either in the daytime or at night. There have been rumours that our friends back in the middle ages were not always overly tidy. At least, we see, they are clearly open to the suspicion of having slept in their underwear.

The story of nightgowns abounds in confusions. As in the past what we think of as day clothes were worn at night, so, too, there have been periods when the matter seems to have been the other way around. Murray's "English Dictionary," after first defining "nightgown" thus, "A loose gown specially used for putting on at or during night in place of the ordinary clothes," continues: "2—A kind of gown worn by ladies in the 18th century, originally as an evening dress." So, it is discovered, one might be unnecessarily startled to read in an old play or novel some such statement as: "She appeared before the company resplendent in her nightgown." The lady, likely enough, was quite elaborately clothed.

The same lexicographical authority further proceeds: "3—A light garment worn in bed, more specially one worn by women and children." And by this we are reminded that in our grandsires' day, before they became "night-shirts," men folk slept in nightgowns. Then, the popular advent of pajamas, or, as the Englishman writes it, pyjamas, for men—and more recently for the feminine world.

To what extent pajamas have entered the feminine world is here a pertinent subject for inquiry. They have not, those who live by women's wear state, appreciably affected the business in nightgowns. They are used extensively for negligée, rather than for sleeping; in certain circles of the younger generation are called "smoke suits." Many industrious souls have found that at home they can work better in them than in ordinary attire. Is their vogue mainly a fad or is it a real development in the history of dress? One prominent "factor" in the women's wear trade reports that the sale of pajamas has decreased during the past year from that of the several years directly preceding.

CHEMISE OR NIGHTGOWN

To come back to the subject of the length of nightgowns. Esmeralda in Victor Hugo's "Notre Dame," you will remember, had a very short shift. In fact, this resulted in her being arrested as a bad character. Since that day the length of that garment has apparently been steadily increasing. But, as was shown at the outset of this outline of nightgown history, nobody knew just what the authentic length should be. Now the matter is determined by decree. No, a new Amendment to this effect has not been slipped into the Constitution.

There is an organization bearing the name of the United Underwear League of America. It is interesting to find that its home is in a former temple of bibliophiles, the old Grolier Club building. One who enters there now, however, with the expectation of finding manikins strolling about and displaying the latest and loveliest things in feminine underwear will be disappointed. Information, but not illustration, will be furnished him. An affiliation of organizations dwells under this roof, United Waist League, United Petticoat League, United Women's Wear League, maybe others. They are all working for the same general ends, the elimination of waste in manufacture and the protection of the public and the buyer for the retail store. A prime way in which this is to be accomplished is by the standardization of certain details of the wearing apparel with which they are concerned. The idea is a fairly new one. It had its spring in considerable measure in the conservation required of us during the war. These organisations began, in this building, six years ago. They are in close co-operation with the fashion makers of Paris. In fact, Paris has come to adopt many of their promulgations.

Nightgowns are cut according to the piece from which they are made, which has a standard width of thirty-eight or forty inches. The manufacturers who are members of the United Underwear League recently put a committee to work to determine, among other things, the soundest way for this to be done. So now, after the uncertainty of the ages, nightgowns, except those of very low price, are all approximately of one length—when you buy 'em.

IX

SOME PUBLICITY FOR THE ENDURING MASTERS

THE other day along came another one of these literary questionnaires. There seems to be no end to the interest in them nowadays— lists of the "ten" books one would choose for various reasons, "shelves" and "libraries" of divers characters. There seemed to me to be more than usual point in Frank P. Adams's notion of the books which he felt it would be most profitable for him to take with him to "a thickly populated archipelago." That is an exceedingly nice question for anyone (so disposed) to ponder.

I cannot explain how on earth it has been that I have not before this examined into the matter with an eye to a list, but I have just now risen and looked over my own "bedroom shelf." And it occurs to me that in comparison with the many others I have seen detailed it has a certain freshness and novelty. As possibly a matter of some interest to any "shelf" hounds who may chance

[83]

upon these rambling notes, let me jot down the titles of a few of the intimate "bokes" I find at my "beddes heed." From left to right the outstanding volumes appear to be these:

THE HOUSE ORGAN—HOW TO MAKE IT PRODUCE RESULTS. By George Frederick Wilson.

PARTY LEADERS OF THE TIME. By Charles Willis Thompson. 1906. Inscribed copy.

THE TRUTH OF CHRISTIANITY. Compiled from Various Sources by Lt.-Col. W. H. Turton, D. S. O., Late Royal Engineers.

AIREDALE SETTER AND HOUND. With a Chapter on The Pointer and Irish Setter. By Warren H. Miller.

ABE MARTIN'S ALMANACK. By Kin Hubbard. 1906. Inscribed copy.

MANUAL OF THE AUTHORS' CLUB. 1918.

WHEN WINTER COMES TO MAIN STREET. By Grant Overton. Inscribed copy.

HYDRIOTAPHIA. Urn Burial: with an account of some Urns Found at Brampton in Norfolk. By Sir Thomas Browne. Half vellum. London: 1893.

THE HUDSON-FULTON CELEBRATION. Catalogue of An Exhibition Held in the Metropolitan Museum of Art. 1909.

SPIERS' AND SURENNE'S FRENCH AND ENGLISH PRONOUNCING DICTIONARY. School Edition. 1907.

THE BOY GREW OLDER. By Heywood Broun. Unbound sheets.

BAEDEKER'S LONDON AND ITS ENVIRONS. 1911.

But enough. If that "library" does not contain the "essentials" of a miscellaneous education—well, then I don't know a miscellaneous education when I see one. And, come to think

[84]

of it in that light, I really don't know why it should not serve a meditative man reasonably well cast away on a "desert isle." There's a fairly wide range of human interest played upon.

A Princeton university professor would, doubtless, be quite lost (so to put it) cast away on a desert island without books. And a number of these gentlemen have, in response to a recent inquiry conducted among them, given us their ideas concerning what you might call a desert island shelf. A New York newspaper has, with considerable perspicacity I think, pointed out that in their highly intellectual interests they have one and all omitted the classic volume which should be of the most practical service to a solitary island sojourner, the hand-book, indeed, of the situation—"Robinson Crusoe."

Nobody, apparently, is out of the range of literary questionnaires at present. A gentleman connected with the Hippodrome, it seems, recently made a canvas among show girls as to the ten best books for a castaway. The response to this of one of the chorus misses in "The Dancing Girl" at the Winter Garden has very much struck me. One obtains in her reply an illuminating commentary upon the status of literature as it presents itself very probably to a large part of the world. "Who wants to read on a desert island?" inquired this lively lass. Her idea is that there would very likely be a lot of *real* fun there, playing with "a sheik" and eating cocoanuts. "No," she declared, "there would be no reading for me. It would interfere too much with the *enjoyment of life*." (Italics mine.) The enjoyment of life is one thing, we discern, and the reading of books something else again.

Myself, it "gets me" how people can knock off so readily all of these lists rating books, authors and other great men. It would seem as though one simply took out a fountain pen, looked down one's nose a moment, filled out the questionnaire, and returned it by the next mail. As Mr. Brentano does not (so far as I know) get up any castaways' steamer baskets of books, if I should undertake to lay out a small group of volumes to keep me company in solitude for a span of years I'd probably miss my ship. I'd put in (first thing probably) "The Home Book of Verse," and then I expect I'd begin to get into difficulties right off. Shakespeare certainly, I'd suppose, ought to go. And the Bible, of course. My old, old friends Benvenuto Cellini, Rabelais, Montaigne, Boswell's "Johnson," "Tristram Shandy" and "Lavengro" would, of course, take my eye. But then (I'd feel) I should need to stop to think over this matter. There's the "Odyssey," and "Don Quixote," and goodness knows what all. Perhaps, when it came to a pinch, I'd really prefer to substitute my cherished "Anatomy of Melancholy" for Boswell. And, indeed, wouldn't that old back-log of my reading, "The World as Will and Idea," hold a lot more for me in the circumstances of my exile than a picaresque tale like "Lavengro?" Wouldn't Casanova be a more spirited companion even than Cellini? What about "Moby-Dick"? It would be hard to be parted from "Religio Medici," which has been at my hand for so long a time. Maybe, alone with eternal things, the mind would care to dwell altogether in the region of Plutarch, Plato and Marcus Aurelius. Anyhow (I reflect), it would be just like me to no more than get comfortably settled on a desert island than I'd discover that I had failed to bring along the books I really wanted there. It's not unlikely that I'd have a great itch to read again, say "Tom Sawyer," or something like that.

My eye, as I pause for a moment from the labor of composition, rests upon a corner of the shelves in my living-room. What do I see there? The two volumes of "Swann's Way," by Marcel Proust, recently translated from the French. Next to this, the two volumes of "The Legend of Ulenspiegel," by Charles de Coster, also recently done into English. Both books lately acquired, and which I mean to read—sometime. I feel it in my blood that, however different in character they may be, both books are very much my kind of thing, so much so that in the complete satisfaction of reading either one of them the process would be (to borrow a turn of phrase of Mr. Belloc's) the incorporation of the work with myself. And there are other books like that on my shelves. But when—at what distant day—will I get around to them? Ah, me! looking through a desk drawer not long ago I came upon a little bulk of memoranda headed, "Books to Read." These notes I had for long forgotten; but I remembered acutely, as I scanned the list, with what eager sincerity with myself I had noted down these titles. There was Herodotus; I had just a taste of him at one time; and I was not long in deciding that I'd go through him from beginning to end—the first chance I got. But in the continual press of multitudinous (and probably lesser) affairs he got lost from my mind.

Burton Roscoe has told us that he is "saving" Dickens for his old age. And a good many of us, I hazard, have in perhaps a nebulous way a notion of books which we are holding in store for sometime later on. None of the ardent list makers seem to have thought of it, but why wouldn't it be a good idea for one theoretically a prospective castaway to see how excellent a list he could make of the enduring books which he has long intended to read and never has read? Perhaps he would become so much interested that he would get at reading some of them without further delay. (Myself, I have just now determined to begin Herodotus day after tomorrow, which is Sunday.)

Another point I have mused upon concerning the lists of the desert islanders is this: all art meet for the sustenance of the soul of man is not comprised in literature. Personally, it seems to me sometimes, as my length of days increases, that great painting wears better even than great literature, that is that one can more constantly (I fancy) have recourse for renewal of spirit to this or that first rate painting than to this or that first rate book. I pause (to take a chance instance at hand) every day or so, I think, for refreshment before my print of *"L' Embarquement pour Cythère;"* I should by no means every day or so take down Congreve. Probably that is not an apt comparison; however, I'll merely leave the suggestion where it is and pass on. If a man of fair intellectual perception should find himself on a desert island with only *one* book, he would be reasonably rich in contact with things of the mind if that were a volume of the drawings of William Blake. I think (you see how complicated the matter becomes with me) I'd have to include in my island kit Michel's "Rembrandt," or something like that. With endless leisure to contemplate beauty and to muse upon the course of civilisation, another book that I should want by me is this folio:

WHITE ATHENIAN VASES IN THE BRITISH MUSEUM, by A. S. Murray and A. H. Smith. London: Printed by order of the trustees. 1896.

I am afraid, however, that it is a work which would be somewhat difficult for a swimmer to salvage from a wrecked vessel, as it is about four feet in height and of the weight of a number of pounds.

Though I am a poor hand to be called upon to reply to a literary questionnaire, and get it in in time to appear in any "symposium," I read with as lively an interest as anybody, I guess, all the lists of this kind which I find. Their currency, I suspect, is productive of considerable good. They should do a lot of log-rolling for genuine genius which doesn't receive the publicity of volumes just off the press. And one should find it a heartening thing to see so much disputation over masterpieces other than those of the moment.

The questionnaire which betrayed me into this rigmarole of thought had a peculiarly challenging turn to it. It was headed (as accurately as I can recall it), "Books Which Have Most Interested Me." The affair went on to say that you were not to vote merely for the books which you acknowledged to be the "greatest," but you were candidly to name those in which you yourself had found most interest. You were not restricted to the field of pure literature; you might put down any kind of books: garden books, cook books, hymn books.

There was something of an implication about this that your private taste might not be one with your conventional professions abroad. There seemed to be a suspicion that you were inclined to declare the superiority of "Hamlet" over everything (because you thought that was the thing you were supposed to do) and then go home and revel in "Snappy Stories." Encouraged, however, by this questionnaire to give a boldly independent answer, and the challenge to complete honesty laid upon me, I looked into my heart very carefully.

In the nature of the thing, a sound list of ten books chosen from the wealth of the world's literature is pretty much restricted to what in the parlance of the painter are called "museum pieces," that is compositions on an exalted scale. And one courts the charge of a perverse taste who should affect to prefer continually works of minor repute to the unassailable masterpieces. Nevertheless, it is a fact which no sensitive critic will dispute that not infrequently some slighter and more spontaneous performance of a master has more intimate interest than his most ambitious work. I suppose the point I am seeking to get at is that the matter of literature is not so simple as one might gather from a survey of our popular literary lists.

"Vanity Fair" and "Henry Esmond," for instance, do not (I should say) settle Thackeray. Myself, as I recall the rapturous days when I first walked into the land of Thackeray I remember the intense enjoyment I got from a book which receives no publicity at all, and the immense admiration I had for it. Who reads, I wonder, "Barry Lyndon"? Somebody of considerable consequence as a critic (I vaguely recall), was it Saintsbury? held it to be in its way the finest of all of Thackeray's books. An early work, belonging to his period of extravaganzas, there is, at any rate, a dash and go to it which he does not exhibit elsewhere, an amazing, driving energy, a superb mockery, a gorgeous romantic glow.

Without in the least presuming to dispute Macaulay's eloquent, if somewhat turgid, allusion to "Tom Jones" enduring beyond "the palace of the Escurial and the imperial eagle of the house of Austria," for the purpose simply of entertainment I much prefer the father of the English novel in the comparative undress of "Joseph Andrews." If I were writing a bit of ad-

vertising copy for Mr. Fielding's publishers I
might say that the adventures of the delectable
Parson Adams is as rollicking, fragrant, tender
and manly a tale as one could find this season.

It has, I am afraid, been a good while since
I have chanced to reread that volume upon which
the greatest Englishman of his time expended the
treasures of his wit, and into which he instilled
the concentrated essence of his rage, "Gulliver's
Travels;" but every now and then I take down
a volume labelled "JONATHAN SWIFT: Historical and Political Tracts—Irish;" and I
turn to that incomparable piece of irony, "A
Modest Proposal, for Preventing the Children
of Poor People from being a Burthen to Their
Parents or Country, and for making them Bene-
ficial to the Publick."

The author of the first instant best-seller, and
as well-known a book perhaps as there is in the
world, was a very industrious man who wrote a
number of books of a good deal of power in addi-
tion to his forever popular masterpiece. Most
of us, I fancy, feel that we have no further concern with Daniel Defoe after having absorbed
"Robinson Crusoe" in our youthful days. "Moll
Flanders" in its realistic erudition remains un-

equalled even among the modern naturalists. And "Captain Singleton," to my mind, is a tale of adventure which is as good reading today as numbers of those which are in the show-windows.

Christopher Morley not so long ago happened upon Boswell's "Tour of the Hebrides," and, in a journalistic pæan, with his own infectious gusto, extolled its flavoursomeness over the monumental "Life." As to the matter of that I do not happen to be prepared to comment. A book which certainly is one of the out-of-the-way curiosities of literature (though I should be very far, indeed, from recommending it as an introduction to Hazlitt) is "Liber Amoris, or the New Pygmalion," "a history," as Mr. Le Gallienne calls it, "of one of the many strange aberrations of genius." I well remember one day when Samuel Butler's "Way of All Flesh" was first becoming known to the American public James Huneker's observing (to W. C. Brownell), "But the *real* thing is his notebooks." They were then only to be consulted in manuscript in the British Museum. The volume later made from these note-books, I submit, is one which any sensible man should be able to feed upon off and on for years. I have a great fancy myself for note-books, wherein thoughts are shot as they fly. And if I should be called upon to compile a list of titles for a shelf of such volumes (no bad idea, it occurs to me) I should early in the matter note down my treasured volume, "Leonardo Da Vinci's Note-Books," arranged and rendered into English by Edward McCurdy.

Among the books of modern authors, too, I repeatedly feel, there are books least read which are far from being the least interesting, indeed, in a case now and then are almost the author's best work. But this ramble, which has only sought to suggest the fallacy of a tabloid view of literature, approaches its prescribed end.

X

IN a very pleasant book recently published there is a highly entertaining chapter on the kind of books universally considered appropriate as gifts for the young in the early years of the nineteenth century. Uplifting the youthful character, particularly the female character, was assuredly the chief concern of those who made such presents in the 1830's and 1840's. Some of the most popular of the volumes designed for this purpose outwardly presented the effect of the ornamentation on a very swagger coffin. And this was fitting enough. One of the most flavoursome volumes of the day opened with a piece by the editor, one the Reverend Mr. Everest, called "The Old Man's Grave." The authors of this colourful literature were, indeed, more often than not, ministers of the gospel. Among other titles of the period, presumably much in demand, were: "The Presbyterian Evenings'

[97]

Entertainment," "Sermons to Young Women,"
"Two Short Catechisms, Mutually Connected,"
and "Woman's Worth; or Hints to Raise the
Female Character." The lately published book
which contains this chapter is diverting throughout. It is called "Books in Black or Red," and
is by Edmund Lester Pearson. And it would,
by the way, make an excellent gift for the youthful character today, a modest present, say, to a
young graduate.

There is a subject which needs some discussion—books as Commencement gifts. It is a subject which appears to be in a woful state. As
a matter of fact, the atmosphere still prevailing
very generally about the matter of giving books
as Commencement presents has to a not incon-
siderable degree the flavour of the quaint days
of the middle 1880's. It is a matter which needs
furbishing up decidedly.

When a person goes to any one of the dealers
in such things and announces that he wants to
get as a Commencement gift a wrist-watch or
a string of pearls, or an automobile, or a fountain
pen, the dealer's eye (I fancy) lights up with
agreeable interest. He does not expect to have
to mull around and fish up something in the style

of his grandfather's time. And when a newly blown young graduate receives as a Commencement present a wrist-watch, or some such thing, that young person's eye, too (I fancy), lights up with agreeable interest.

But (I have observed) very commonly when a person goes into a book store and says he wants to get something as a Commencement present the book salesman's face takes on a weary look. And I strongly suspect that not uncommonly when a youth or a maiden today receives a book as a Commencement gift his heart, or hers, does not leap as though he or she had beheld a rainbow in the sky.

Commencement, one might think, would be a season which holds a peculiarly happy opportunity for the gift of books. It is a festival which celebrates a fragrant achievement of the mind. In England, I am told, this significance of the occasion is much more generally recognised than is the case with us. The practice of giving books as presents at graduation is fairly current, and it is a custom long established. Special editions are got up. I am not acquainted with these special editions of which I have heard, and so I do not know how far they may be in advance of our ideas in general on the subject of books suitable for Commencement presents.

When we examine a bit into the situation with us we find it by and large a lifeless sort of affair. The reason why the bookseller commonly has such a trying time with the customer in search of a Commencement gift is that the customer's ideas in the matter are likely to be pretty rigid, his conception of the range of literature appropriate to his purpose decidedly narrow. He wants, naturally, to give something of enduring value. His thoughts are inclined to run to works of moral and spiritual benefit. Above all things, he wants to be quite safe in his judgment. Should (we'll say in fancy) a surviving copy of "The Presbyterian Evenings' Entertainment" be shown him he probably would regard that as a bit old fashioned, and on the other hand, something deep within him (I am heartily glad to believe) would cause him to suspect a new-fangled work entitled "A Young Girl's Diary," or something by a person of the name of James Joyce called "Ulysses." He wants to select something that he knows something about.

Bartlett's "Familiar Quotations," Palgrave's "Golden Treasury," "Idylls of the King," Mat-

thew Arnold, Longfellow, Keats, sometimes
Pater, Thoreau or Jane Austen, and, in the case
of youths, Kipling—this is the type of presentation book, any bookseller will tell you, most generally sought for Commencement. Now the
principle behind such a quest, of course, is altogether sound. The things, quite properly, to give
are what I have heard called "key books"—something to start one off in life and with which one
may abide. But the trouble with things of the
kind just listed is that, in general, to the minds
of the young they are apt to seem pretty flat.
It is necessary today to have lived some time in
the world before one comes around to the understanding, say, that Tennyson was a fine poet.

Now let us try for a little constructive criticism in this matter. What would be a really
fortunate book for a young person of eager mind
to receive at Commencement? First and fore-
most, I think everyone who deals in books
would agree in naming "The Home Book of
Verse" (Holt). There are two editions, one in
one volume, the other in two. The book is handsome in cloth, and it is, of course, even more
handsome, and durable, in fine binding. Then
there are the sterling volumes of the series which

began with the publication of "The Oxford Book of English Verse" (Clarendon Press). Newer, not quite so standard, but with an engagingly fresh touch among anthologies, is "The Le Gallienne Book of English Verse" (Liveright). Two very suitable volumes, of fairly recent publication, are the critical anthologies, "Modern British Poetry" and "Modern American Poetry" (Harcourt), both edited by Louis Untermeyer, with instructive notes.

If one has a mind to stray from the established classics in poetry there are, of course, any number of pleasant things to be found; though we may here glance at but a few. There is not need, perhaps, to remind ourselves of the books of Joyce Kilmer (Doran). A felicitous gift, I should say, would be the "Collected Poems" of Walter de la Mare (Holt). Certainly one could not go far wrong in selecting Christopher Morley's "Chimneysmoke" (Doran), with its delectable illustrations by Thomas Fogarty. There are editions in several styles. And a book of a number of years ago which, I should say, would be a very acceptable little token is the "Poems" of Austin Dobson (Dodd, Mead). For a young graduate of especially advanced literary interests the complete collection of the "Poems" of Alice Meynell (Scribner) might be considered.

A good idea, it seems to me, is to stimulate the young person's regard for books by placing in his way, or in her's, books about books. With Mr. Pearson's new volume (Macmillan) we opened this little talk. A. Edward Newton's several excellent volumes (Atlantic Monthly Press) have certainly contributed very widely to a quickening of interest in acquiring first-rate books. They are handsomely made, and so decidedly presentable as presents. I know a very accomplished bookseller who has on occasion recommended as Commencement gifts the two volumes of Quiller-Couch, "The Art of Reading" and "The Art of Writing" (Putnam); and apparently with satisfaction to his particular clients, though books somewhat academic in manner. The name of Andrew Lang is a taking one with all children; as they come more into maturity they should have a ready welcome for his enduring adult volumes, "Essays in Little" and "Letters to Dead Authors" (Scribner), and a long line of others. Stevenson's "Familiar Studies of Men and Books" should here not be forgotten. One of the most delightful volumes of literary studies there is to be found, and a book which should be much more read than it is, is Henry James' "Partial Portraits" (Macmillan). It is very easy reading. A companion volume to this is the author's "French Poets and Novelists;" a book which, however, is a little more advanced. As a number of the volumes just mentioned are rather slight in size, perhaps it would be desirable to present a couple of them together. A recent book of very modern and stimulating literary appreciation is "Our Best Poets, English and American," by Theodore Maynard (Holt). Myself, as a stripling I wore to shreds stray copies which heaven sent me of the bookish writings of Augustine Birrell; and to this day I hold that there has been no more enchanting literary essayist within the present century. A handsome set of "The Collected Essays" and "Addresses" of the Rt. Hon. Augustine Birrell, 1880-1920, three volumes, has just been issued (Scribner). The volumes are not sold separately.

A very charming kind of book, I think, is the anthology of letters. They are excellent in giving one a little taste of a great deal, and, perchance, of luring one on to fabled fields. One likes to keep them about near at hand for years, and to dip into them every now and then. An admirable little volume of this sort is "A Letter Book," edited by George Saintsbury (Harcourt). Another, of later date, is "The Gentlest Art: A Choice of Letters by Entertaining Hands," edited by E. V. Lucas (Macmillan). And to this there is a companion volume entitled "The Second Post." A highly agreeable type of volume somewhat akin to the anthology of letters is the literary miscellany, in which a connoisseur of literature has lovingly assembled a bouquet of extracts from his reading. Good examples of books of this sort are "The Ladies Pageant," edited by Mr. Lucas (Macmillan), and, an earlier volume, "A Bookman's Budget," "composed and compiled" by Austin Dobson (Oxford University Press). The lively, personal, contemporary essay of more or less literary quality being decidedly in vogue at present suggests an anthology which should be welcomed by any young graduate; "Modern Essays," selected by Christopher Morley, with informal introductory notes to each author (Harcourt). An affair of considerably more extensive sweep

[105]

is the set, "Modern English Essays," 1870-1920, in five small volumes, edited by Ernest Rhys (Dutton).

A book which over and over again I have seen given with much success as a graduation present to young women is "The Lady: Studies of Certain Significant Phases of Her History," by Emily James Putnam (Putnam). It is a very fine book, indeed; and of engaging appearance. An excellent work which I should think would be treasured by a graduating miss is the volume "Etiquette, In Society, In Business, In Politics and At Home," by Emily Post (Mrs. Price Post), (Funk and Wagnalls).

There are, of course, all sorts of sets, big and little, costly and moderate in price, of Shakespeare, Lamb, Stevenson, and so on, many of them in limp leather. In Jane Austen, by the way, I have always fancied the little edition with the coloured pictures by Brock (Dent). If one is seeking something without regard to cost, and quite in the spirit of our time, I might suggest an investigation of the recently issued Seawood Edition of the books of Booth Tarkington, in sixteen stately volumes (Doubleday). One should follow, of course,—though in the selection of books as Commencement gifts it seems this frequently is not particularly done—the individual taste of the young graduate. It might be that the most fitting gift would be a volume of enduring worth on painting, on music, architecture, interior decoration, bric-a-brac collecting, or on something else.

XI

THE NOBLEST COOK-BOOK OF THEM ALL

A WAITER known to Delmonico *bons-vivants* for some thirty-six years bent over me, one (as it is written in fame) Crispi, in private life Battista Ravera. Polished in manner, he, as waiters are not in the days on which we have fallen. An aroma of distinction about him. No wonder. Has he not known through the length of many years the best society of an aristocratic *régime* that is no more?

It was a ferociously hot day. But as I sat in a rear corner of that restaurant room, perspiration running in rivulets down my back and legs, I felt cool and very pleasant in my mind. My eyes rested upon (and caressed) the eloquent words:

All white wines must be served cold.
Sherry and Xeres cool.
Bordeaux between fifty-five and sixty degrees, Fahrenheit, according to its growth.
Burgundy between fifty and fifty-five degrees.
Champagnes, cold or iced, or in sherbets.
Dessert wines cool.

[108]

THE NOBLEST COOK-BOOK

My soul came back to me amid a flight of dreams. My spirit was uplifted and refreshed. But there (alas! and alack! and some more alases!) is where I brought up—with purely visionary refreshment. Never again (as far as we can foresee today) will the excellent Crispi reply to a noble-hearted wine order with: "Yes, sir. Very good, sir."

You see, it was this way. An old-timer, who wrote to his newspaper an Epicurean's lament at the passing of Delmonico's, remarked that if the former patrons of that gastronomic institution of old Knickerbocker days would duplicate the delectable creations served there let them seek a book complete in every detail for the reproduction of these viands, compiled by Delmonico's former *chef de cuisine*. Now that was a matter worth looking into. So off I set.

For books, naturally, a book store. I laid my course for Charles Scribner's sumptuous emporium. But the most distinguished bibliophiles there shook their heads. They recalled indistinctly such a work as a Delmonico cook-book, but it was no more, "out of print." They looked into the archives, handed down from generation to generation among those that are book men—

nothing listed under the word "Delmonico." But wait, here was the name cited by our communicative epicure, Charles Ranhofer. He had, it was recorded, on a time put together a volume called "Epicurean Cook Book." But it was not published by any regular publishing house, had been issued by some sort of a concern listed as "Caterer," maybe a magazine. In fine, the book was not readily available, a stray copy might be picked up in some old-book store.

On a thought, I turned down to the corner that had been the illustrious Delmonico's. A great (and hideous) hoarding was up on the façade, and, I noted, the auction was on. I entered the one time august portal. Within was dissolution. Things were about in every which way. There was much litter in that but yesterday immaculate precinct. Money changers swarmed the temple.

At the direction of a functionary at the door, I mounted to the second floor. Increased disorder. Winding through the press I pushed toward the continuous sound of a lifted voice rising and falling. In a spacious rear apartment a straggling knot of persons was gathered in one corner about the elevated figure of the gesticulating auctioneer. Throughout the fairly populous room generally, however, interest in the sale under way seemed to be decidedly apathetic. It was, the detached observer felt, altogether a rather ribald looking throng to be gathered under this classic roof. There were any number of young men who looked as if they might have something to do with pool rooms. A somewhat humorously pleasant note was given to the scene by the presence every here and there of a quaint old lady of a Humpty-Dumpty style of architecture. The intruder waylaid a man crossing the floor without any hat—everybody else had their's on—and stating his errand was directed to the "office," on the first floor.

Here the caller was told by a very affable young gentleman that, yes, "Sabatini" had the book. He? The erstwhile Delmonico *chef,* now down at Robbin's, on Broad Street. The young gentleman offered the inquirer a cigar and said he would telephone down. Sabatini, it developed, had the book at home; he would bring it in, in the morning. Sabatini did not sound to the seeker quite like Ranhofer, but there could be no doubt that in the offing there was a cook-book associated with Delmonico's.

Early on the morrow the cook-book trailer arrived before the neat yellow ochre front of the S. W. Robbins Company restaurant, with its trim row of iron lamps, its graceful iron fence and balcony, in the curve of Broad Street. An *attaché* of the place summoned Sabatini from his station below the ground floor. Pending his arrival the subject of the visit was, in a slender measure, discussed. Yes, this young man (maybe the manager) said, it was a good thing—that Delmonico's closed. How was that? Well, the place was an old fashioned idea, old fashioned *menus*. Don't serve that way any more. Nowadays quicker. Gentlemen in high hats no more. Golf togs now, up in Westchester County, or over on Long Island. Why, twenty years ago Wall Street was full of high hats; now a gentleman wearing one—people would look at him!

A huge figure in shining white cap and apron loomed up the stairway from regions below, face very round, smooth as an infant's, very pink. He advanced with a rolling tread, a massive redbound book resting in his hand. "Isn't he a picture?" ejaculated the Robbins young man. He certainly was. He came to rest at our table with somewhat the effect of a great ship being

warped to at her pier, and I was presented to
the noble Sabatini. An expression of remarkable and child-like innocence pervaded his coun-
tenance. He said, in reply to the question, that
he had been *chef* at Delmonico's for four years.
Ah! Ranhofer, he was back some time ago. And
Sabatini laid the great and precious tome before
me, an astonishingly thick quarto volume, of (I
later noted) 1183 pages.

It was, I perceived, a presentation copy from
L. M. Boomer, manager of the Hotel McAlpin,
inscribed: "To Sabatini Nicolas, with many com-
pliments and best wishes. The Lenox, Oct. 28,
'09." An engraved frontispiece portrait presented the bust of a sturdy man, of a distinctly
French cast of features, with a grey moustache.
The title-page was a marvel of ornate decoration, as elaborate almost as an illuminated missal
of the early centuries. The design, an old fashioned wood engraving, presented a border of
richly laden grape vines and of flowing ribbons,
interwoven with various fruits and ears of grain.
Just within this, at about the middle of the page,
looked out the heads of an ox and a deer. Below
this, at one side, a representation of a banquet
hall, and, at the other side, of a vast kitchen.

Within the border, along the bottom, game and fish and domestic fowl, with divers vegetables scattered about here and there. Somewhat above the centre of the page, a cut of "old" Delmonico's. The words of the title-page read:

THE EPICUREAN

A Complete Treatise of
Analytical and Practical Studies
on the
CULINARY ART
Including
Table and Wine Service, How to Prepare and Cook
Dishes, an Index for Marketing, a Great Variety
of Bills of Fare for Breakfasts, Luncheons,
Dinners, Suppers, Ambigus, Buffets, etc.,
and a Selection of Interesting Bills
of Fare of Delmonico's from
1862-1894
Making a
FRANCO-AMERICAN CULINARY ENCYCLOPEDIA
BY CHARLES RANHOFER
Formerly Chef of Delmonico's
Honorary President of the "Société Culinaire
Philanthropique" of New York
Illustrated with 800 plates
New York
R. RANHOFER, Publisher
782 West End Avenue, New York

The volume was dedicated "to the memory of Messrs. Delmonico." A fac-simile reproduction of a letter in long hand followed the dedication.

[114]

THE NOBLEST COOK-BOOK

The printed letter-head read: "Established 1827. Office, Beaver and South Wm. Sts." It was dated: "N. Y., Feb'ry 24th, 1893." The script began, "Chef Charles Ranhofer, Esq-re;" and it concluded, in reference to the book: "A perusal will, I think, give one an appetite, Yours truly, Charles C. Delmonico." The preface contained, among others, the following paragraphs:

The book is divided into twenty-four chapters:—Table Service, Bills of Fare, Supplies, Elementary Methods, Soups, Stocks, Hot and Cold Sauces, Garnishings, Hot and Cold Side Dishes, Shell Fish, Crustaceans, Fish, Beef, Veal, Mutton, Lamb, Pork, Poultry, Game, Miscellaneous Entrées, Cold Dishes, Vegetables, Cereals, Hot and Cold Desserts, Pastry, Bakery, Confectionery, Ices, Fruits, Wines and Preserves.

Not relying solely on my experience and knowledge, I have quoted from the most illustrious modern author, my much beloved friend and colleague, Urbain Dubois, ex-chef at the Court of Germany, and it gives me sincere pleasure to thank him for his generous assistance.

The profession will acknowledge its indebtedness to the Messrs. Delmonico for the interest shown by them in developing the gastronomic art in this country.

Many will recall the business receptions given to distinguished guests under the supervision and direction of Delmonico's.

Mention may be made of the following dinners: to President U. S. Grant, to President A. Johnson, to the Grand Duke Alexis of Russia, to General Prim, to Charles Dickens, to Sir Morton Peto, to August Belmont, to Giraud Foster, to General Cutting, to Luckmeyer, the so-called "Black Swan Dinner," to Admiral Renaud, to Professor

Morse, to Bartholdi, to De Lesseps, to the Comte de Paris, also the ball given to the Russian Admiral and Fleet, and the Greek dinner.

Sabatini and the young man of the discourse on high hats had withdrawn; now another figure paused beside the cook-book student, an elderly, an ancient, waiter, bent and gnarled. He eyed the book with bright curiosity. "Is it— 'The Epicurean'?" he deferentially asked, with a very pleased inflection. Now drew nigh another, he who later was revealed as none other than Crispi. Had they known the *chef* Ranhofer? was asked. Oh, yes; many years. What sort of a man was he? Big, very big, strong. What became of him? Died, long ago. They shook their heads with happy reverence: he was down at the old place, William and Beaver Streets; went up to Forty-fourth Street in ninety-seven; in 1903 it was, they thought, he left. How long altogether had he been with Delmonico's? They cudgeled their brains, these two old chaps. One figured that it was upward of twenty years. But Crispi hazarded that it was nearer forty.

Then they fell into musing reminiscence. "Twenty-sixth Street, that was the place," murmured Crispi, with a fond, fond sigh; "that was the *cream*." Then, "prohibition's what's done it at last," he said, gloomily, and moodily moved slowly away. I was looking through a section of *menus* in the book. Each *menu* was headed by the name of a month, thus:

JANUARY—BREAKFAST

Oysters with lemon
Eggs on a dish with cèpes
Broiled fresh codfish with bacon
Calf's head vinaigrette
Hashed pheasant
Porterhouse steak à la Sanford
Saratoga potatoes
Pèlerine tartlets
Dessert

The ancient waiter explained: "People used to eat in season. Don't any more. Asparagus now any time. Hot-house stuff." And he grimaced, as though to say, "Bad doings." I turned to "June," to see what in earlier Knickerbocker days gentlemen regarded as a seasonable and satisfactory breakfast. The first menu I found for a Spring morning was this:

JUNE—BREAKFAST

Omelet à la Andrews
Bluefish, Havanese style
Calf's brains in matelote
Baked potatoes

[117]

Clams, Philadelphia style
Chicken roasted in the saucepan
Watercress and apple salad
Baskets filled with oranges.

How about a snack in the middle of the day. At random, here is one:

JUNE—LUNCH

Lobster à la Delmonico
Timbales Mentana
Mutton cutlets with chicory
Artichoke bottoms, Montglas
Croquettes of capon à la Royal
Coffee, cream éclairs
Cherries

Let us glance at the ritual of dinner, as the estimable Ranhofer understood it. As the guests arrive they are shown into the reception room.

In the reception room there should be a small Russian buffet, or simply serve some sherry, Xeres, bitters, vermuth and absinthe, to be handed round on trays to each guest as he arrives.

The formal etiquette prescribed of "going in" to dinner is too extensive for our space here. Next matter treated of is "Table Service *(Dinner Service à l'Américaine et le Menu);*" and the first thing therein considered is, "Service of Wines and Cordials *(Service des Vins et Liqueurs).*"

The steward must inform and specify to the butler the wine to be served at each separate course. However important the dinner may be, still decanters of ordinary red and white wine must be placed on the table. The selection of the finer wines is the host's duty, he making his choice when ordering the bill of fare.

The steward's duty is to see that the wines are served at a proper temperature.

A specimen wine service is then presented. There is the "First Service," and wines are named to go with oysters ("The butler will pour out the Chablis, stating the name of each wine he serves"), after the soup, with fish, with removes, with *entrées* ("Iced punches and sherbets, rum Madeira"). The "Interval," then the "Second Service" ("Should there be no ladies present, cigarettes can be handed round at the same time"): wines to go with roasts ("Serve Burgundy from bottles laid flat in baskets (Fig. 767) holding the basket in the right hand a white napkin in the left"), with cold roasts, with hot desserts. "Third Service:" with dessert. Then, wine liquors, cordials, beers.

Lists are given of "Wines and Liquors Usually Called For *(Vins et Liqueurs Généralement Servis)*" at a dinner of Frenchmen, of Germans, and so on. For old time's sake and the heady flavour of a bygone age let us record one.

[119]

LITERARY LANES

A Dinner of Americans

Reception Room

Sherry   Bitters   Cocktails

Dinner Wines

Haut Sauterne	Amontillado	Sherry	Barsac
Pontet Canet	Perrier	Jonet Brut	Liquors

At the conclusion of the dinner:

It is now time for the hostess to bow, push back her chair and prepare to rise, this being a signal for the ladies to retire; after they have returned to the drawing-room, coffee is passed round on a salver containing spoons, hot water, sugar and cream. A few moments later another waiter comes forward with an empty tray to remove the cups the ladies hand him.

The gentlemen partake of their coffee in the dining-room; at the same time serve them Kirsch, brandy, chartreuse, cigars and cigarettes. The doors are closed and the ladies and waiters have retired so as to allow the gentlemen more freedom to talk among themselves, still it will be necessary to enter the drawing-room and dining-room occasionally in order to see whether anything be needed so as to avoid being called as much as possible.

After half an hour or so, the gentlemen will rejoin the ladies in the drawing-room and then tea is served. . . . After the tea the service is considered to be ended.

The distinguished author of "The Epicurean" observes: "Gremod de la Reyniere has said that, 'No one ages at table;' he might have added, when the dinner is good and the wines are of the

[120]

finest. Wine is the intellectual part of a meal."
He has this to say as to how to make coffee:

It takes three kinds of coffee to obtain a good result:
for instance, Mocha for the aroma, having it only slightly
roasted, Maracaibo for the colour, which should be well
roasted, and Java for the strength, roasted to a degree between the other two.

An extensive section of the volume is devoted
to recipes. A number of them are hardly adapted
for use in an ordinary household, as, for instance,
instructions for the preparation of a green turtle
weighing one hundred pounds, and such recipes
as those for bear steak broiled, boar (wild pig)
tenderloins, and pheasants adorned with their
own plumage. Partridge with sauerkraut, and
baked thrushes, sound attractive. Interesting if
not altogether practicable for most of us is this:

Volière Galentine of Pheasants à la Casimir Périer
Procure two fine English pheasants with handsome
plumage, remove the skin with the feathers from the neck
and upper breast, also the wings and tails, being careful not
to destroy their natural beauty. Fix the heads in such a
way that they retain their natural appearance, etc., etc.

Throughout many pages, however, are given
recipes which should be of active interest to the
domestic reader. From among them the following selection is gathered:

LITERARY LANES

Chicken Fricassee with Curry

Divide two small chickens of a pound and a half each, after cleaning well, into four distinct parts; pare them well. Put two or three spoonfuls of chopped onions in a saucepan and fry with butter till of a fine colour; add the pieces of chicken, toss them for two minutes and season, sprinkling two dessert spoonfuls of powdered curry over. Moisten to their height with stock, put in a pinch of parsley garnished with thyme and bay leaf. Peel and chop up a small sour apple, add it to the chicken and let cook over a slow fire, taking out the fillets as soon as they are done, then remove the legs, place them in another saucepan with the fillets. Strain the sauce and reduce it with a few spoonfuls of good raw cream and as much mushroom broth. Take it off the fire, thicken with three egg yolks diluted with cream and a piece of butter divided into small pats. Dress the chickens, cover over with sauce and serve a vegetable or dishful of Indian rice.

Veal Cutlets with Fine Herbs

Cut, pare, beat, and season six or eight veal cutlets; put them into a sautoir containing butter, fry them on both sides over a brisk fire, and when well browned, drain off the fat into another small saucepan, and lay it on one side. Moisten the meat with a little stock, let the liquid fall slowly to a glaze in such a way as to finish the cooking, and lastly add a few spoonfuls of white wine. In the fat put aside, fry colourless two or three spoonfuls of stuffed shallots and onions, with five or six spoonfuls of chopped up new mushrooms, and continue frying until these have lost all their humidity, then thicken with a half glaze sauce. Let this cook for a few minutes, and pour it over the cutlets in the sautoir, besprinkle with a few spoonfuls of chopped truffles and cooked ham, and let simmer together for seven or eight minutes. Dress the cutlets garnished with frills on a long dish. Add to the sauce a pinch of chopped and blanched parsley leaves, pour it over the meat.

[122]

THE NOBLEST COOK-BOOK

Delmonico Sirloin Steak of Twenty Ounces, Plain

Cut from a sirloin slices two inches in thickness; beat them to flatten them to an inch and a half thick, trim nicely; they should now weigh twenty ounces each; salt them on both sides, baste them over with oil or melted butter, and broil them on a moderate fire for fourteen minutes if desired very rare; eighteen minutes to be done properly, and twenty-two to be well done. Set them on a hot dish with a little clear gravy or maître d'hôtel butter.

Blue Fish à la Barnave

Select very small blue fish weighing half a pound; clean, wash and wipe them dry. Fill the insides with a pike quenelle forcemeat, into which has been mixed a quarter of the same quantity of cooked fine herbs. Range the fish on a buttered baking dish, sprinkle over some butter and cook in a moderate oven; when done dress them on a mushroom purée and serve a separate barnave sauce, at the same time as the fish.

Trout, Stuffed

Draw four trout by the gills, each fish to weigh half a pound; wipe well the insides, and fill the belly with a paste made of fresh butter, white bread crumbs, parsley, onion, and mushrooms, all chopped. Season, then roll each one in a separate sheet of oiled paper; lay them on a baking dish containing melted butter, and let cook for fifteen to twenty minutes in a moderate oven, turning and basting frequently. Wrap and dress them on a dish, serve with their own butter and slices of lemon ranged round in a circle.

Bisque of Lobster

Plunge into boiling salted water twelve pounds of small, live, well washed lobsters; cook them for twenty-five minutes; then drain; break their shells and extract all the meat. Pound the lobster meat with its equal quantity of boiled rice; season with salt and red pepper, then dilute it with fat broth or lean, should the bisque be desired lean, strain through a sieve, and again through a tanny. Heat it up without allowing it to boil, add a pint of béchamel and half a pound of lobster butter; stir well the bisque until the butter is thoroughly melted. Colour a lobster bisque a deeper red than the crawfish. Crusts of brioche a quarter of an inch square, and dried in the oven, may be served at the same time.

POTATOES, PARISIENNE

Cut them with a three-quarters of an inch diameter vegetable spoon, fry slowly in plenty of hot fat, and when three-quarters done drain this off and lay them in a sautoir with clarified butter, toss, season with salt, sprinkle over with chopped parsley and serve.

FRIED EGGS WITH BROWN BUTTER

Break four or five eggs into a frying pan containing some hot butter; scald the yolks with the butter and cook until glossy; season, remove carefully with a large skimmer and lay them on a dish. Put more butter into the pan and when slightly brown without burning strain it over the eggs; put a little vinegar in the frying pan and pour it over the eggs through a strainer.

PARSLEY OMELET

Parsley omelet is often confounded with fine herb omelet. Use only eggs, seasoning and chopped parsley. Chop up some very green fresh parsley, put it into the corner of a napkin and dip this in several waters, remove the cloth at once and squeeze out all the moisture. Break eight eggs into a vessel, add the parsley, also pepper and salt. Melt some butter in a pan, pour in the beaten eggs and set it on the open fire; move the pan rapidly with the left hand, using a stew-spoon in the right hand. When the omelet is done fold it on both ends, turn it over on to a dish and shape it prettily.

THE NOBLEST COOK-BOOK

Strawberry Short Cake

Place in a basin six ounces of butter with ten ounces of sugar; beat both well together until a creamy preparation is obtained, then add three eggs, one at a time, two gills of milk and vanilla flavoring. After the whole has been well mixed pour in a pound of sifted flour into which has been added a coffee spoonful of baking powder. Have some round flat moulds seven and one-half inches in diameter and the edges raised to three eighths of an inch high; butter and flour these over, then fill them to the top with the mixture and bake in a brisk oven. Unmould on a grate as soon as they are done and leave stand till cold; cover each one of the layers of cake with a vanilla pastry cream and on it arrange very fine ripe strawberries, one next to the other, bestrew with sugar and lay two of these garnished cakes one on top of the other. Put on a dish, cover the cakes with sweetened whipped cream, flavour with vanilla and push through a pocket.

Meringue Peaches

Cook half pound of rice in milk, finish with cream and butter. Cut six peaches in four, remove the kernels and plunge them into boiling water until skins peel off, then drain on a cloth and cut them up into small quarters; besprinkle over with sugar. With the cooked rice form with a spoon any style border, leaving a hollow in the centre; inside of this dress the quartered peaches in layers, brushing them over with apricot marmalade and alternating with thin layers of the rice; the whole to be covered with the rice and this with a layer of meringue. Smooth the surface, decorate with meringue, dredge with fine sugar and dry in a slow oven for twenty minutes.

Water Cress and Apple Salad

Have very clean and green water cress; season it only when ready to serve with a very little oil, salt, pepper, vinegar and some sour apples cut in slices.

The dish rhapsodised by the gentleman who wrote in to the paper is this:

CANAPES LORENZO

Fry colourless two ounces of onions cut in one eighth of an inch squares, and when done add a tablespoonful of flour; let this cook for a few minutes without browning, then moisten with a pint of fresh cream; season with salt, cayenne pepper and nutmeg, and reduce it to the consistency of a well thickened sauce; now throw in one pound of crab meat sautéd in butter over a brisk fire in a pan, letting it boil up once and then set away to cool. Cut slices of bread a quarter of an inch thick; from it cut round pieces four inches in diameter, using a cutter for this purpose, divide them straight through the centre to make two even sized pieces of each, toast them on one side only, cover this side with two ounces of crab meat for each half round; and lay the following preparation on top: with the hands work in a tin basin one half pound of butter, add to it grated Parmesan cheese, cayenne and white pepper and knead these together adding grated Parmesan so as to form a thick paste; cover the entire canape with a layer of this butter and cheese and set them on a buttered baking sheet in a hot oven so they attain a fine colour, then serve them as quickly as they are removed from the oven. They may be made round shape two and a half inches in diameter if preferred.

The book being returned, with many thanks, to Sabatini in his handsome kitchen below, he said: "Glad to have met you."

XII

THE ROMANCE OF TEXT-BOOKS

WHEN the series of articles called (in the magazine) "The Practical Side of Writing" was concluding its serial publication in *The Bookman,* and when this material was being reprinted in the form of the book called "The Business of Writing", a couple of letters were received by the authors of the chapters suggesting that some consideration of the business of text-books be included in their work. Had these friendly suggestions been received earlier this would have been done. At the time they came along, however, it was too late to fit an article on this subject into the order of the series winding up its appearance in the magazine, and the book was already going through the press. The matter of how text-books come about is quite a story, and one known hardly at all. And so I here offer to anyone interested a little discussion of the subject.

The field of the text-book is a little world of its own. Text-books are conceived, written, edited, and marketed in a way which is quite unlike the production and distribution of books in general. The whole business has undergone a very interesting development within recent years.

In the "old days," as the text-book publisher puts it, text-books were written much as any sort of a book probably is usually supposed to be written. That is, the author went ahead and wrote it; he put into the book the fulness of his knowledge of the subject upon which he was engaged just as he felt it; and when he had completed his manuscript he duly submitted it to a publisher. Changed has been all that.

The field today is thoroughly plotted. The text-book publisher keeps pretty close tabs on the whole field of potential authors of text-books: anyone engaged in the work of education who is likely to have up his sleeve a book on his subject is fingerprinted, so to say, by the educational publishers. And he is more than liable to be annexed by some publishing house before he gets very far in his work of authorship.

The publisher and the author frequently work

very close together in the production of a text-book; often they might almost be called collaborators in the authorship of the book. For instance, the writer of a text-book does not commonly sit down and, as the author of another kind of a book often does, simply put forth his own mind on the matter. It is customary for him to carefully consider what sort of a book of the kind appears to be particularly needed at this time, what seem to be the short-comings of the volumes in current use in this department of instruction, what features which would be an improvement upon them could be devised, and so on. And in his contact with his publishers, as the work of writing progresses, the book oftentimes is very considerably shaped this way or that by the counsels of the publishing house. Further, after a manuscript has left the hands of the author, it is every now and then the case that the amount of editing it receives (with, of course, the acquiescence of the author) alters quite appreciably its earlier form. Cases have been where text-books have been practically re-written in the publisher's office: the publisher wanted a book *by* a certain teacher, instructor or

professor, but found he did not want it at all
as the manuscript came to him.

Publishing of the general sort is, of course, a
good deal of a gamble. Books which the publisher "banks" upon with a feeling almost of cer-
tainty every now and then fail to go over; books
for which he expects only a moderate sale, every
once in awhile go "big." He turns down books
which later are published very successfully by a
rival house; he bids in books which never get "out
of the hole." The element of chance is always
present to a considerable degree in publishing
an author's first book. In text-book publishing,
however, the hazard is reduced to a minimum. In
general publishing, in the main, the publisher
must rely practically altogether on his judgment
of the possibilities of the book; beyond that he
shoots pretty much into the air. But in the text-
book business the publisher may focus his aim
upon a definite target; he is able to make fairly
precise calculations. The standing of this or that
educator, briefly to illustrate the matter, would
make reasonably certain the use of his book in the
college or university where he is a member of the
faculty; the many students he has had who have
become members of the teaching staffs at other

places would fairly well insure its adoption, in at least a number of cases, in their classes, and so on. In short, the territory is, with something not far from sureness, charted; in the life insurance term, the "expectancy" of a text-book may be more or less mathematically determined.

Now and then one hears it darkly intimated that the "real money" from writing is in textbooks; the rewards from a popular novel are all well enough in their way, but the author of a successful text-book or two has no end of a goldmine. Well, in this as in other matters the textbook business is peculiar. To begin with, the educational book business is not subject to anything like the periodical depreciation of fortune incident to business conditions generally which is the common lot of any other kind of publishing. Text-books are not luxuries but bread. During the widespread business depression of 1921 or thereabout, a period of decided severity for the book trade generally, I recall that the educational publishers with whom I am acquainted were the only publishers I know who continued in good spirits. Indeed, I remember, they bore not a trace of worry. Houses which combine a general list with an educational list apparently sus-.

tained quite easily the precarious course of their general business by the steady keel of their educational business. And then in times of national prosperity it appears that there is a greatly increased popular appetite for education, and consequently a more voluminous distribution of text-books than in ordinary days.

The active life of most books is brief. They haste away quite soon. One season is the span of even a very successful book, a book of fiction or of general character. After its little hour on the stage its sales steadily decline, in most cases practically cease altogether after so long a time as a year. With educational books it is not uncommonly the other way around. I was told the other day of a text-book which had been going for seventeen years; some time ago it had a sale of twenty thousand copies a year, last year its sale was a hundred thousand. That, of course, is rather an exceptional case; but in practically all cases text-books are "property books." They have something of the character of durability of a piece of real estate. They are revised again and again and continue to sell year after year.

Among the peculiar things about the text-book business is this circumstance. A book (we'll say)

[132]

of clever, humorous essays becomes advertised all over. It has a very merry vogue. Reviews of it are all around; columnists feed on it; "everybody" talks about it; everyone, pretty literally, has heard of it; the author's picture is published broadcast; he is regular famous. The book, doing exceedingly well, sells maybe between ten and fifteen thousand copies. Right along, text-books which, so to put it, "nobody ever heard of," sell as well as that, not during one year only but for a number of years running.

Such things, indeed, have happened as an instructor in a small college, with a salary of perhaps twenty-five hundred dollars a year, waking (as the romantic term is) to find himself the recipient of royalties amounting to maybe twenty thousand dollars in a year. Similar things have happened in various fields of effort, but nowhere do we find them happening every day; and many authors of established text-books are persons of incomes modest enough.

The highest percentage of royalty is paid on books of fiction, where a very fair royalty is twenty per cent. of the list price. The usual royalty on books of non-fiction ranges from ten to fifteen per cent. A sliding scale of royalty is the customary arrangement—ten per cent., say, on the first thousand copies sold, and fifteen per cent. on all copies thereafter, or something like that. Authors' royalties on text-books do not differ materially, I should say, from the royalties on non-fiction books in general. But there is this fact entering into the matter of the author's returns: text-books frequently sell for very little. Ordinarily a person inclined to buy a copy of a celebrated book of memoirs, or a widely acclaimed volume of travel, or something like that, is not over-likely to be deterred from the purchase by finding the book to be fifty cents more in price than he had supposed. Indeed, (I have heard it said in the book trade) a person who is willing to pay six dollars for a book frequently would "just as soon" pay ten. That, doubtless, is not invariably literally so, but it is quite true enough for the purpose of the illustration here. Now a difference in price of as little as a cent between two competing text-books has sometimes swung the balance in favour of the adoption by a school-board of one over the other. Text-books are for those mostly with "but litel gold in cofre."

Not a little work on text-books is done for

very slender pay. Introductions oftentimes are written by invitation for school editions of the classics, for instance, and the volumes edited for an amount something like the space rates paid by the more or less literary magazines for an article. The plan ordinarily followed, it seems, when a series of books for educational use is prepared is for the general editor, the editor of the series, to receive the royalties, the editors of the various volumes each being paid outright a nominal sum for his work. This practical simplification of what otherwise would be a highly complicated matter, sometimes, when the series becomes a very substantial property, works out in a way which may seem unjust to the associate editors. But, after all, the initial *idea* was that of the general editor, his the prime constructive thought—and the associate editors were invited to be, not coerced into being, associate editors, and, usually in such cases, had expressed themselves as happy in the arrangement when the deal was made.

An entertaining bit of publishing history which could have happened only in the department of educational books is this. When the author of any other kind of a book enters into an agreement with his publisher to deliver his manuscript

on a stated date he usually gets it there within
something like hailing distance of that time. It
would be a remarkably grotesque thought to him
to suppose that he might send it around sometime after the arrival of the next generation.
William James, however, in delivering the manuscript of his "Psychology" was eighteen years
late.

In publishing houses which combine a business
in educational books with a general publishing
business, the educational department customarily
refers to the whole of that part of the business
not educational as the "trade department." This
practice is confusing to one whose connection
has been with a house not having an educational
department, as there is meant by "trade department" that part of the house not editorial, nor
manufacturing, but which has to do with selling
the books—which deals directly with the *trade,*
the booksellers. When, however, we look a bit
into the educational publishing business we see
the logic of its use of the term "trade department." Another one of the peculiar things about
the text-book publishing business is that *it* doesn't
deal with the book trade at all. And so consequently one in the educational department of a

publishing house quite naturally thinks of that part of the business engaged with books which are handled through the booksellers as, in distinction from his field, the trade department.

Every publisher, of course, has a staff of men whose business it is to go out and obtain orders for his books, his salesmen, or travellers. In the case of the regular publishing business these are men whose entire lives have been passed in the atmosphere of business, commercial dealing. Many of them have grown up in the book trade, starting in as "list boys," lads employed by bookstores to fetch from the publishers books which have been ordered by customers and which have been found to be out of stock. They wouldn't be successful as editors, any more than editors would be likely to be successful as salesmen. They are frequently paid considerably higher salaries than the editorial workers in a publishing house. They go out on the road with their cases of samples and deal with the "buyers" of the bookstores. A publisher's success (and the success of his authors) is in no small degree in the hands of his salesmen.

Buyers for bookstores are as a class people who have spent their lives in the book business.

They are as a rule very much the same sort of capable business people dealing in books that publishers' salesmen are. Both speak the same language, that of the "trade." The "travellers" for an educational list live in another world, have another language altogether. When you talk to them (or, at any rate, when I talk to some of them) you might think that nothing went on in the world except schools, colleges and universities. They have it all laid off that way in which the race is divided up into "Yale men," and "Harvard men," and "Cornell men," and so on. If you happen not to be one of any of these various kinds of men, you are likely to experience a feeling that you are not any sort of a man at all. The gossip of the regular book travelling salesmen, naturally, is all of the book trade, the general publishing business, and of authors more or less popular. They tell of how this buyer has gone from a store in Indianapolis to one in Los Angeles, of how that publisher is shaping his business, and comment on the changed allegiance of a certain well-known author from one house to another. All of this seems simple enough to one whose field has been the general book business. To him the gossip of the text-book traveller is marvellous; it seems wonderful that he should know apparently everything that happens to any kind of an assistant professor anywhere in the country. But that, precisely, is his *business*.

The ranks of educational book travellers are recruited in some measure from the field of teachers. Occasionally it happens that a man who has been a teacher, and has become a text-book traveller, later returns to the teaching profession. He is in very much the same atmosphere all the while. Whether or not they have ever been teachers the main body of them are, in the fullest meaning of the term, "college men." And in their own world there is specialisation. Among text-book travellers there are, for instance, "high-school men," as distinct from the representative of college text-books.

The business of educational book travellers is to circulate around among the schools, colleges and universities; they have no concern with book-stores. Their personal friends are largely among the teaching staffs of educational institutions. They call upon them, and visit them; are entertained by them, and entertain them. A general publisher has a large corps of travelling salesmen when he has five or six; but a going educational list is likely to be represented by twelve or fifteen travellers. Though text-books are very little advertised, even in educational journals, the overhead of marketing them is decidedly high.

The text-book traveller knows thoroughly the books he handles. He can expound to his hearer exactly why the book of which he speaks is (in the opinion of its publisher) superior to other books of its kind now current. He can follow through the book he has in hand page by page, illustrating point by point its peculiar features as compared with the methods employed by other volumes. He is familiar with the machinery of education.

His course of procedure, in the case of a school-book, is to endeavour to obtain at such-or-such a place the approval of as many teachers as he can; then he goes to the principal for support of the volume. Sometime before the matter of adopting a new book of this character is likely to come up before the board of education, or trustees, or whatnot, he puts forward the claims of the volume to members of that body. On the day, and the day or so preceding, the sitting of this tribunal the publishers' representatives of divers rival volumes turn up in the community, and a form of lobbying becomes entertainingly active.

The teachers and the principal that the text-book man has been able to "get" stand him in very good stead, as nowadays the question of the adoption of a school-book rests very largely upon their attitude in the matter. In the "old days" the situation was more picturesque. It was frequently an affair of decidedly low-brow and cut-throat politics. In those jocund times some school-book publishers used to maintain pleasant relations with local town characters of personal popularity. The postmaster, say, might receive a small annual retainer. He was likely to know nothing whatever about text-books, or books of any other kind. But when the time came around for the public officials charged with that office to consider new school-books for the district, it was his concern informally to put in his oar. "Now looky here, Ed," he might say, "this means something to me." Or he might say it in another way. But, as I observed, those were other days, and other ways.

XIII

ONE time in the long ago—on October 13, 1906, to be quite exact—the *New York Times* was provoked to comment sarcastically on a style of book illustration very much current at that period. It was in the heyday of that stuffed affair known as the "gift book." Of the making of elaborately illustrated editions of every conceivable classic of literature there was no end. Masterpieces, great and little, were illustrated at all hazards, and as often as not with comical inappropriateness. The editorial commentator in the *Times* cited as especially wonderful instances of lack of discrimination, the selection of E. W. Kemble, popular as a delineator of the Southern darky, to make drawings for the "Vicar of Wakefield," and of Elizabeth Shippen Green, who had gained her following by her sentiment in her drawings of children, to illustrate the "City of Dreadful Night." Hardly

[142]

anything, of course, could have been more preposterous. There were other examples galore
almost as ludicrous. One in particular that the
memory cannot lose was the set of drawings commissioned of Howard Chandler Christy for a
de luxe volume of poems by James Whitcomb
Riley. But the book-buying public of the time,
or, at any rate, the very considerable and apparently insatiable gift-book-buying public, evidently was not perturbed a jot by the phenom-
enon of a group of aristocratic New York types
comporting themselves as natives in the neighbourhood of the ol' swimmin' hole. Performances
of that kind could be counted on for a great run.

And then, maybe a dozen years or so ago, the
huge vogue of the "art book" of this order began
to wane. Perhaps, in the natural course of
things it was on the road to wearing out its welcome. People, it may be, had begun to have
enough of such contraptions. At any rate, with
the war the flood of elaborately illustrated books
of all kinds went out. Highly difficult manufacturing conditions made such volumes too expen-
sive a publishing venture. Books of value to
the discriminating student were for awhile in
eclipse as well as the erstwhile merely popular

[143]

picture volumes. Latterly, with the return to better publishing conditions, the illustrated book on a fairly sumptuous scale has been coming back. What, one may inquire, is to be its general tendency in this new day?

We are all very much aware of our literary Renaissance. The serious biography has supplanted in popular favour the hack writer's spurious concoctions which of yore loaded the fashionable bookseller's tables, "George Sand and Her Lovers," and all that kind of thing. Poetry of intellectual content, the literary essay, criticism, fiction of searching social analysis, of course, are upon the town, and our old friend Pollyanna and her kith and kin are nowhere. Most happily, the trend in recently published books going in more or less lavishly for illustration has been decidedly in an auspicious direction. These volumes have been mainly *bona fide* art books; not art books of the rather superficial type which prevailed a good deal in the gift book days, a fancy affair of much picture with a trimming of gossipy text, but the ambitious productions of the historian and the critic; such excellent and enduring volumes, for example, as the exhaustive folios on the work of the

[144]

Adams, by Arthur T. Bolton, curator of the
Soane Museum; the rich and comprehensive work
on "Subjects Portrayed in Japanese Color
Prints," by Basil Stewart; the study of "Goya as
Portrait Painter," by Beruete y Moret, the late
director of the Prado; the worthy memorial volume to J. Alden Weir, and the monograph,
"Honoré Daumier," with manifold reproduc-
tions and sympathetic essays by several hands—
books published, by the way, all within a few
months, a year or two ago. And, by the by,
another outstanding book of quite authentic art
for which we were indebted at about the same
time is the ever delectable Max Beerbohm's
"Rossetti and His Circle." So the times yield a
fair enough profit for the student and the ama-
teur of art, the collector awake to what he is
up to.

But there are signs, too, that in the world of
embellished books the millennium is not yet at
hand. The publisher today has indicated in a
way heartening to those concerned for the matter
his confidence in the support of a very fair body
of book-buyers who are, to some degree, at least,
connoisseurs. And there is, in contrast with
more florid publishing days of the past, an agree-

able absence of "colour books," and other such truck. But roundabout here and there in the new era one begins again to come upon a threatening survival of the most woful ideas in illustrated editions of works of literature. And is it not one's bounden duty, when he knows them for what they are, to view with alarm the possibility of their return each coming season in greater numbers?

The reason why such senseless book illustration continues to be possible may be illuminated by what we may call a parable. One time not long ago a person who in youth had thought to be a painter and who had directed his early education toward that end was talking for several days with a very distinguished poet in his home, one of the very first in rank, indeed, of our poets; a man of the most lofty artistic conscience in his work, firmly holding to exacting standards of craftsmanship, detesting the faintest breath of the meretricious and the shallow in literature, his life a persistent pondering of the varying aspects of beauty which he feels around him. On his wall, handsomely framed, the visitor observed the original drawing of an "illustration" which had been used in one of this author's own books of poems. It was so wretchedly feeble as to make the visitor squirm in his chair to look at it.

With, obviously, a feeling of cheerful approval for the lamentable thing, the poet got it down for his friend's closer inspection, and unsuspectingly asked him what he thought of it. Polite, evasive murmurs, his friend felt, in the presence of a nature of such intense sincerity would have been a shabby way out of the situation. And so the matter was frankly taken up—the matter of the appalling discrepancy between the character of vitality of the author's own work and the total emptiness of the "decoration" made to accompany it, to (shall we say?) "interpret" it. This very sagacious man of pungent verse didn't require to be hit on the head with a marline-spike to get the idea; when (at last) he really looked into that picture he saw that there was nothing there at all.

A perception of the principles of decorative art does not "come natural." It does not even necessarily "go along with" a very careful belle-tristic education. I have known very celebrated Oxonians whose comments (innocent but firm) on "art" would drive a painter into something like delirium tremens. Any number of people who are in familiar contact with literature have little or no insight into the work of the painter and the draughtsman. Paint and line do not talk in the selfsame language as literature.

An uncommonly high and sensitive intelligence in any art is not at all incompatible with a very decided "blind spot" in regard to another. Painters are not in general noted for their discernment in matters of literature. Nor actors, nor musicians. Indeed, a good many of them (anyone, I think, will say who has lived among them) do not read, to speak of, at all. But a painter (we'll say) does not, usually, "set up" to be an arbiter of taste in literature. A critic of literature would probably dismiss his judgment if he should presume to do so. At any rate, there would not be enough of his kind to affect the course of a work of literature.

On the other hand, I quote from a letter of the other day from an esteemed book-loving friend of mine, "it is quite true that it seems to be more or less generally assumed that if we have something of an instructed and cultivated taste in literature we are, *because* of that, equally sensitive to art." Of course, it is an old, old quarrel between the literary man and the painter. Art is long and this article must be brief. The point of my friend's letter for the discussion in hand comes here: "I frankly admit that I am a perfect dunce as an art critic. I wouldn't think for a minute of posing as such. I do, however, think I know something about *book illustration.*"

He then goes on, it should be added, to tell of the books he has collected for their drawings; and they turn out to represent no dunce-like array of art at all: Rowlandson, Cruikshank, Leech, Rackham, Hugh Thomson and Beerbohm. But an excellent text he has left with us—the notion that it doesn't matter whether you are concerned with the principles of some kind of fine art in museums and galleries, to have good taste in book illustrations. Bad illustration is frequently furthered by cavalier dicta handed down by some of our favourite book commentators; just the other moment appeared such a happy-go-lucky compliment paid to the decorative designs made for a mediæval romance of wide publicity, which æsthetically have utterly no business there. Editors of publications of excellent literary quality again and again reproduce in the pages under their control illustrations nowhere in keeping with the cultural sophistication of their text—drawings which, if they should see them as they see poems, they would very summarily have thrown out. And in justice to book publishers it should be said that some of their most peculiar offerings in the way of picturefied editions of this and that are not inspired solely by an avaricious hope for quick sales. They are not unlikely to think that the stuff is all right.

Not a bad way to come to some appreciation of any art is to realise how bad some of the worst of it is. One of the most deplorable failures in illustrated editions is one of the most persistent. More often than not the kind of books set upon are precisely the kind of literature most difficult of all for pictorial art to reflect. There was, indeed, nothing so incongruous about William Blake's setting about to make a series of designs for the "Book of Job." And Hans Holbein was in his sphere when he turned for the moment to the illustration of the "Old Testament" and the "Dance of Death." We need not be aghast at Delacroix's seeking (with questionable success) to interpret "Faust" and "Hamlet." And though Doré's grandiloquent mannerism fell far short of the "Inferno," there is a certain amount of

logic in the combination. But such a thing (and
it is liable to appear any moment) as an edition
of the "Book of Job" illustrated by a young lady
entering upon study in the life class at the Art
Students' League of New York *is* more than
likely to be decidedly worse than senseless.

A small army of illustrators of varying talent
have at one time and another essayed the "Ru-
báiyát," but who has had the peculiar genius to
catch the spirit of the magic of Omar Khayyám?
Nearly all of the decorated editions are very
bad. Frank Brangwyn made the poem an excuse
for a set of colourful posters. Elihu Vedder,
doubtless, came nearest to the spirit of the Per-
sian philosopher, and is the standard. But, to
my mind, he is pretty prosaic. I seem to feel a
decided lack of wine in his nature.

Now, it takes something more than a little
talent to create a picture, which has any value to
it, of such a thing as, let us say, Morning in the
Bowl of Night flinging the Stone that puts the
Stars to Flight. The common resource of the
journeyman illustrator who has the cheerful
temerity to attack the symbolism in works of
literary genius is vagueness. And when he leaves
everything, so to say, up in the air, he is pretty

[151]

sure to be complimented here and there upon
having his work "full of feeling." In fact, this
lack of clarity, which is thought by some to be a
mark of the "imagination," is much more apt to
be the mark not of imagination but of the absence
of it. The more far-fetched the literary image,
the more precise in the hands of a great artist
generally has been the presentation of it. There
is no feeling about blindfolded in a mist in the
actually sublime "Apocalypse" woodcuts of Al-
brecht Dürer.

Many a profound masterpiece of literature reduced to a bare outline of its concrete action
would be but a sorry story—and that precisely
is what popular illustrated editions often have
made of them. Edmund J. Sullivan, himself an
illustrator of distinction, in an excellent volume
for the student, "The Art of Illustration"
(1921), cautions his reader to be diffident of
undertaking to make an illustration for the line:
"O Absalom, my son, my son!" Dramatic
gesture alone is untrue. The drama of a broken
heart becomes (in another way) more heart-
breaking still when travestied by gesticulating
hands, extended fingers and protruding eyes.

It is a familiar thing to find a literary work

of lofty moral or lyrical exaltation accompanied by a set of what may correctly be called costume plates, where what happens more than anything else is that the characteristic magic of the work begins to evaporate as soon as the *dramatis personae,* in the dress of the period, are bodied forth to the eye; the drawings convey nothing more than the illustrations of a melodramatic novel, since maybe the work, although perhaps among the classics of poetry, *is* nothing more or less than a novel, where the narrative is given impassioned form. The novel is emphasised and the lyricism or fervour expelled, the mediocre husk alone remaining.

But enough of this side of the matter. The best way to come to an understanding appreciation of any art is to cultivate an acquaintance with the best that has been done in it. Books were illustrated from the beginning. Erudite interest in finely illustrated books has resulted in various public and private collections of noteworthy examples. A memorable collection which exemplified book illustration at its best throughout four centuries was assembled in the print gallery of the New York Public Library in 1919. An instructive little essay called "The Illustrated

Book," by Frank Weitenkampf, Chief, Arts and Prints Division, being his "notes" on the exhibition prepared for the Library *Bulletin,* and reprinted together with several illustrations, may be had of the Library for a very nominal charge. Uniform with this, and likewise to be obtained, is a valuable pamphlet by Dr. Weitenkampf entitled "Illustrated Books of the Past Four Centuries," a record of the exhibition in the form of a catalogue elaborately annotated from many sources. Dr. Weitenkampf is the author, too, of a very useful little, historical volume called "American Graphic Art," issued by a New York publishing house in 1912, which contains a chapter on our book illustration. And, all in all, the illustrative work of America is in many ways perhaps more interesting than that of any other country; at least Mr. Pennell has asserted that it is.

Though the supreme classics of literature have not always fared well at the hands of the illustrators they have repeatedly engaged the powers of men of genius. The Dantesque illustrations of Botticelli presented a conjunction of two spirits which enriched the world of art with some enchanting designs, and gave stimulus to the analysts of the poet; but the idea of the need for the artist to adjust his design to the conditions of the printer was of later date. The independent pictorial interpretation of a great literary theme, even when successful from the literary or artistic point of view, is not logically an illustration, even when bound into a book by means of "inserts," or other devices. That is a very important point which has not been achieved by many illustrious artists: the illustration should comport in perfect harmony with the printed page.

The history of book illustration from the earliest times follows, of course, the history of the development of processes for reproducing decorative designs; and the art finds an expression not only in the individuality of the artist, but, naturally, in the group individuality of the nation or race. An Italian classic of the fifteenth century changes its colour with the cuts redrawn in a French edition of the sixteenth century.

A very rapid survey of the field of outstanding modern book illustration may have its uses. The Pre-Raphaelites, Rossetti and Millais, appropriately lent their hand to the illustration of the Moxon "Tennyson" (1857), which introduces

the group known as the men of the "Sixties."
In this group was included Charles Keene, who
stands as the equal of any of the world's master
draughtsmen; and a representative body of
whose work has been gathered from the pages
of *Punch* into a handsome volume, "The Work
of Charles Keene," with the text by Joseph
Pennell (London: 1897). In Germany at approximately this time Adolf Menzel, one of the
greatest illustrators of the century, was employed upon his two hundred illustrations for
the works of Frederick the Great. In France,
in 1863 or thereabout, Doré's "Don Quixote"
and Rabelais illustrations, done with so much
élan, were entering upon their immense vogue—
now gone down the wind. And, a little later, in
London John Tenniel made the forty-two drawings which probably will always stand as the rare
right illustrations for "Alice in Wonderland."

Nothing more exquisitely appropriate can be
found in book illustration than the drawings
made early in the nineteenth century by Edwin
Abbey for Herrick, "Old Songs," and for "She
Stoops to Conquer." If his famous Shakespeare
illustrations express grace rather than dramatic
force or grandeur, he at least did as well as

anyone has ever done. It is to be regretted that
his fellow countryman of the period, Howard
Pyle, though he exercised his distinguished and
versatile gifts throughout thirty years of prominent attainment, did not set himself to some work
which would stand as a particular monument.
In England at about this time a boy of twenty,
Aubrey Beardsley, was lavishing his rich inven-
tion and the resources of his decorative line upon
the five hundred and forty-eight vignettes and
decorative borders which he did for the "Morte
d'Arthur." And a French gift of rare talent
to the art of illustration of the period was the
Boutet de Monvel "Jeanne d' Arc" drawings.
Many lesser though happy unions of pen or
brush with classic text have of necessity in this
space been passed over.

In the infant years of the present century
was issued a work which in high authority is held
to be the pinnacle of book illustration, the Daniel
Vierge edition of "Don Quixote" (1906). In
this overshadowing undertaking the most noted
pen draughtsman of his age, as Royal Cortissoz
observes in his introduction to the volumes,
rounded out his long and active life as though
with a predestined felicity. Throughout his

years he had cultivated the medium of the pen with close reference to modern reproductive processes. Spanish born, Velasquez and Goya his ancestors and true masters, he gives us a brilliant and worthy interpretation of one Spanish master by another.

Would that artist and publisher and general public could in this day draw more together in this matter—the possibilities of book illustration would be illimitable.

XIV

I HAVE just got back from a little visit over Boston way. Unfortunately I have been there but little, and I failed to remember to equip myself properly. I forgot that Boston and its vicinity does not have the mild, dry, delectable winter climate that we enjoy in New York. I went over embellished with a pair of handsome taupe spats. My delicate grey silk tie was unobscured by a muffler. I remember that I used to think (before this trip to Boston) that all these young women who in recent winters have been flaunting these monster galoshes, of more or less Russian effect, just did that to be, as presumably they considered it, fancy. I now regard these articles of apparel as objects of beauty in their season, revealing in their wearers not affectation but wisdom.

Well, after a day or so in Boston, when I got out to Cambridge I gave up any further effort at the New York manner. I borrowed some regulation New England accoutrement from my host's sixteen year old son, and went in for going out right in that setting. But this enlightened course I had adopted too late. I had already acquired a very vigorous all night cough, and upon my return to New York a corps of eminent physicians assembled at the scene of my distress pronounced my attack a very severe case of laryngitis. For a period extending well over a week any attempt at vocal articulation has only resulted in my producing a weird jumble of hoarse rumbles and shrill squeaks. And so I have been quite removed from contact with the active world. I have passed my time in meditation.

The situation has occasioned my meditating upon the matter of one's being removed from contact with the active world. Is there any merit to be got out of such a circumstance? Or is one as hopelessly lost as one at first feels himself to be? With the unaccounted passing of time has come to me a suspicion that perhaps having lost out of the running has its points. I have sometimes had this suspicion, too, (that the world is too much with us) when I have been quite well. It has come upon me at times when I have wandered into the still presence of, say, a Rembrandt. How smaller than nothing was all the excitement about art and literature that one had left a few moments before! Would it not be enough, and more than enough for the spirit, for one to sit here for days, and weeks, in communion with enduring beauty? Would it matter a particle if in doing this one missed altogether the clatter about the most talked of novel of the hour?

Vain dreaming. One is, it would seem, inexorably bound up with one's own day. As to painting, certainly one would not want to have missed, say, Twachtman. And it's one's portion to enjoy in due proportion George Luks as well as Rembrandt. And literature, of course, is a living stream forever flowing on, taking colour and direction from the changing ways of man. No, it will not do to sit down by a shelf of the immortals; is it not one's part to keep one's mind open, too, to the half-gods as they come and go? Even straws may show which way the current flows.

And so the chap who had felt content with a Rembrandt and the world well lost is pretty soon

again caught up into the whirling shuttle-cock
of the moment, reading as he runs. He answers
a letter asking him to recommend a reputable
literary agent. He stuffs himself with literary
paragraphs, concerning the goings and comings
of someone or other who is maybe the author of
a "first novel" said to be about life to-day in a
"prep" school, and another who is perhaps going
to read his verses somewhere next Saturday afternoon. He takes away with him over the week
end more books probably than a very great
stylist, Abraham Lincoln, found need of in a life
time. Not quite the same sort of books however,
all just off the press. And yet down deep at
his heart's core there is a yearning for *something
to read* that is not satisfied. You see, (poor
soul!) he is in the business—by reading largely
he gains his bite and sup—and so he seldom has
time, it seems, to read for (let us say) his immortal soul's sake. It is highly probable, the
thought sometimes strikes him, that he has forever lost that art. He must, very likely, go on
and on in the round of reading what at the moment is being read; and talking about it very
much as everyone else does.

But when he was a very young man how

magical a thing was reading! How incredibly
spacious were those days! He read exactly
where his heart listed, and for the thing itself.
He spent a full year, I do believe, living in the
pages of "The Anatomy of Melancholy;" and
when he had come to the end he began it anew.
How many months "Gil Blas" occupied him I
could not undertake to say. And there, of
course was "Cellini," and "Tristram Shandy,"
and "Lavengro," and others unnumbered. In
each new emprise he added a cubit to his stature.
He read authors clear through, Jane Austen,
Thackeray, Mr. James, at, so to say, a sitting.
Current "literary" columns doubtless were about
in those days, but curiously enough to him they
seemed far away. The din he did not hear,
wotted not of. The shadows were the realities.
Reading was a passion. It sometimes struck
him as a shame that one could not reasonably
expect to live much longer than three score years
and ten, as he would (certainly at the leisurely
rate he was going) have to leave unread so much
in the great treasure house of the centuries. And
yet, after a time, the supply of books in the
world's locker which could hold the spirit so completely in thrall began, it seemed, to run out.

[163]

I know a very intelligent (and a very beautiful) lady who never reads the newspapers, or at least when she does it is intermittently and by chance. She has suggested to me that I "try it" for a period now and then, not reading the papers. She assures me that I would find this experiment very refreshing to my mind, and that I should really "miss nothing." During this season of detachment from my ordinary rounds, which has diverted the usual course of my reading (and put into my head these divers little reflections upon reading in general), I have come upon a point in the matter of newspaper reading which I had not considered before. I have perceived that my reading of newspapers has been pretty much specialised. I had been reading, along with the momentous news of the day, practically only those things which more or less concerned me in my field of affairs. I turned through the paper in the morning and in the evening, perhaps with a little briskness, noted those things which pertained to my orbit, glanced at a front page sensation or two, and passed on to other matters. I was always upset when I missed my particular paper, through some mischance, it might be, connected with going in or

out of town, or something like that. No, I was
willing to admit that it was a highly intellectual
thing to do, but I knew that I couldn't learn to
live without newspapers.

As at this time, then, when my participation
in affairs is in eclipse, I might have thought that
newspapers would have meant less to me than
ordinarily. On the contrary, I find that I read
them hour after hour. I send out for papers I
never read before. I read endlessly matter of
no concern whatever to me in my doings:
"Society," "Ocean Travellers," "Arrival of
Buyers," "Echoes from Readers," "Barometer
Readings," real estate transfers, and so on and
on. I ponder the comic strips to ascertain their
humour. I peruse pages of details about minor
heroes of sport totally unknown to me. Nothing
is too alien to my habitual thought for me not to
pore over it. I read the papers, in short, with
that immeasurable thoroughness with which I
have observed other persons of large leisure read
papers on benches in the parks. I have discovered something about newspaper reading. Now
when you have laryngitis they give you a drug
derived from the poppy, called codeine, or something like that. Theoretically, its beneficent

action is to dull the nerve in your throat, and so diminish the incentive to cough perpetually. Well, among its undoubtable effects is that of dulling the nerves of the brain. It tunes the mind to just the sort of reading I have described. And people who continually read newspapers in that way, as I frequently see them in the subway and elsewhere, I suppose are at the other end of the intellectual scale from the lady who does not read them at all. I shouldn't want to become addicted to that opiate way of reading newspapers, but I fancy that I'll find that the experience for a time has been rather refreshing to me. It carries rest of mind further, I think, than not reading at all.

I recollect that during my visit in Cambridge I saw very little attention paid by any member of the family to newspapers. A couple appeared to be taken in regularly, but the children of the household seemed to be the only ones at all drawn to them. Maybe my host was for a few days taking a rest from newspapers such as the lady recommended for me. As "history in the making," so I believe it is said, is in the newspapers, I should suppose that a distinguished historian and a professor of history at Harvard would to some extent look at them; but, at any rate, it was clear that this gentleman was not a slave to them. And this incident in the matter of newspapers brings me around to the point which I had in mind when I set out to put down these desultory reflections.

I found the discovery rather startling, but it seems that, after all, we do not (the more or less book bred population of the country) all read exactly what the others are reading and talk about it in almost precisely the same way. The lady I have mentioned is a poet; she had quite recently talked and read both in Boston and at Radcliffe College. She is very successful in this activity. My professor's daughter is a student at Radcliffe. It was with something of a shock that I found (in attempting to make light conversation in the way conventional in my circles) that the members of this family were quite unaware that she had been there. I began to suspect that they might not even know that Al Kreymborg was again back home.

As you may now be slightly prepared for such an announcement, I'll mention that "Babbitt" they had not read, nor did they seem to be more than faintly interested in any allusion to the book. No, not a particle, it was obvious, did any of them feel any sort of an obligation to read anything because it was widely being read. Their intellectual position socially, one saw, had been made quite secure in other ways. There were rooms lined with books. The talk was largely of acting, painting, literature and travel. But they were quite untrammelled by transient eddies. One felt in the atmosphere here something of the breath of being at the centre of the thing.

My host, on being obliged to leave me alone for a few moments, got down with a gesture of gusto a portly volume of the essays of Schopenhauer, a recent acquisition of his, in which obviously he had been finding much joy. Ah, me! it was in those days when I was very young that I conned by heart the three massive volumes of "The World as Will and Idea." And here was a man of books, appreciably older than I, who still, it would seem, sits down and revels in something that he reads simply because he wants to— something that there hasn't been a word about in the "literary news" for goodness knows how many years.

Aye, reading in general has got most deplorably to be a very stereotyped proceeding. Literary opinion is very largely manufactured, like political sentiment. A President and a bestseller may come about in ways not altogether dissimilar. And it may be strongly suspected that the seemingly popular judgment returned on a book is rarely a really honest expression of taste.

XV

I

THERE was a cheerful, look-alive and very much up-to-date undertaker. Or rather, he was a mortician, which nowadays means the kind of undertaker I mean. There was also, in that great city, a journalist. Something of a humourist he was, or so a moderate audience of simple-minded readers thought him. At any rate, he was going along one day and his heart was pretty heavy, for his head was quite empty of anything entertaining to make into copy.

Then it was that, by a chance glance, his eye spied an undertaker's "parlour," one of the old fashioned kind, a humble place. For this happening was on a shabby street. In that instant, the journalist's spirit was uplifted, and a lark began to sing in his soul. Undertakers' shops, he said (for his mind was given to levity), are funny places; I'll write an article about 'em.

[170]

This forthwith he did, and afterward thought little about the matter.

But in this world you never can tell, ofttimes a man casually turns a street corner and maybe a month or so later (or after many years) this results in the changing of the whole complexion of his career. It was like that with this journalist. When he was having a little fun with lowly undertakers it didn't occur to him that any undertaker would ever read his article; and, if the thought had struck him, he'd have had a humorous notion that the undertaker would be sore at him.

Now, however, this very-much-alert mortician was not in the habit of missing anything in the papers which had anything at all to do with his business; he read that journalist's smart little piece; and he said to himself (presumably): "Clever chap, that; very readable sort. But he's got hold of the wrong dope; we'll show him the real thing in this line; and we'll get him to write a prize booklet for us, which will make folks all over sit up."

Well, when approached, the writer fellow didn't know; he was pretty well full up with work at the time; and, too, the idea of his writing advertising for an undertaker hit him as considerable of a joke. He didn't take on the job, right off; but after awhile he reflected (you see, it was rather a handsome rate per word that mortician was willing to pay); he reflected, after all, what does an architect do? Why, he designs a jail or a cathedral, doesn't he? according to the requirements made of his talent. And did not the great masters of old paint for Court or Church, as they found in one or the other a patron? Why, then, should not a professional writer write anything, that could be honestly done?

Thus the matter came about. If (as, with a smile, you may say) this booklet was undertaken in avarice, or something akin to that motive, it was not so that it went forward. The writer, his interest as an artist becoming more and more engaged, plumb forgot the money which was to be his hire. He looked over a collection, a voluminous one, of booklets got up for other undertakers; he felt that they were bad, all of them, very; he would do the thing *right,* and once for all.

No one need ever presume to write another undertaker's booklet, he determined; like Millet's

"Sower," the thing would have been done. If you want to laugh, go ahead; but it is no more than a fact that this writer bird went at his advertising booklet, not, of course, with the imperishable genius, but, in its degree, in the spirit in which Henry Bacon pondered his design for the Lincoln Memorial.

And when he had got it done, I will say that he rather fancied the thing. The lively mortician chap was greatly pleased; he had, he felt, put something novel over on the undertaking fraternity. One prime point about this booklet (the result of a problem to which the writer had set himself) was that it rigorously eschewed all the stock words and phrases from time immemorial common to the language of undertaking, now become threadbare, and even ludicrous, from everlasting use. Nowhere in it would one meet up with the terms "bereaved," "deceased," "remains," and so on. It read in a human, natural way.

Time passed along with the journalist. Came to him after awhile an itch, as we say, to look further into this advertising matter. That booklet—begun with the notion that it would be regular hack work; profitable, but more or less of a

bore—had called forth, in a surprisingly stimulating way, his ingenuity. There might be something he could bring to advertising, something
he could find there.

Yes, he would set about to pick up other com-
missions in this line. He'd need to do this, he
supposed, through some of these concerns called
advertising agencies. Consulted several cronies
of his at his Club, made out a list, and started
round. But didn't get far. At first house he
struck—run by friends of friends of his,—when
he had told his tale, it was suggested that he
might best try out his idea by coming into the
organisation. He'd see how he liked it all.

Forthwith, an arrangement quite agreeable
to him was made. . . . And a little later we find
him being asked by his friends all around town:
"Well, how do you like it, the advertising business?" Then, as one after another asked him
this, he perceived that invariably they smiled.
Yes, they seemed to think there was a joke in it.

Here, you see, he was, what you might call a
legitimate writer; indeed, he had something of a
"name;" had been associated with journals of
literary character; had to his credit a string of
books, not without a very fair standing among

[174]

the critical. Himself, he wrote criticism, and
paid especial attention to style. Had been generally regarded as having, more than most, what
is called an artistic conscience. Therefore, his
reaction, from the very inside, to the great American business of bunkum would be, of course—
well, certainly amusing. Was he not, too, a
humourist?

Several of his friends (those, maybe, who most
loved him) seemed to think it rather sad—that
which he had done; his career, it was evident to
them, had taken a down-hill turn. Their letters
in acknowledgment of the news of his new business connection could hardly be said to have
reeked of congratulation. One newspaper para-
graphist was contemptuously ironical in the announcement he wrote: alas! see what he had come
to, our friend; and it showed him up—his real
character—all right!

II

Advertising and the advertising man, it's quite
the fashion among the intelligentsia to slam
them. Distinguished novelists, beloved "colyum-
nists" and knock-about journalists get a great

[175]

hand right along by making game of the advertising business. A mere glance around supplies us with any number of examples of the good work going on. There's "Bunk," by Woodward Boyd; recently in the *New York Evening Post*, "H. B.," in his daily column, "Books on Our Table," said, "We continue to hear that it is a wonderful attack upon the great American institution." Wallace Irwin, in the best novel of his career, "Lew Tyler's Wives," has a lot of fun with an agency; Lew's sensitive and aristocratic wife, of course, is horrified by the crass and awful place. Grant Overton, in his carefully wrought novel, "Island of the Innocent," shows his readers around the low-lived works in an advertising house. Chris Morley grows hilariously satiric in his skit, "The Story of Ginger Cubes." The acclaimed Aldous Huxley takes a deliciously sophisticated fall out of advertising in his novel, "Antic Hay." One of the most recent to pan the business is Roger Burlingame, in his novel "You Too." And there are others all over.

On the stage, the advertising man—bumptious, flashy, a typical "go-getter," humorously obnoxious—is a stock character of comic relief; as standard a figure as used to be the funny

Irishman, with clay pipe and shillalah—and one (timorously) might add—about as easily drawn.

And so what? Well, those who met our journalist friend with that question, "How"——, and so on, doubtless expected some such jolly reply as this: "Oh, boy! It's where the money is. But, holy cat, what hokum!" Instead, it is here to be reported, he said that he found the whole thing exceedingly interesting. More, he thought the advertising business very good for the character. In fact, he felt that it might make a man of him yet. He got a laugh here, but it was obvious, too, that he really was in earnest about something. "How come?" he was asked.

You have seen how he got into this business. He was, perhaps, bringing to it a high-ideals complex, which was going to be given a black eye very shortly, when he had got into the hard-boiled running. He was, after all, in fibre an artist; that is, his nature craved, above everything else, excellence in any product of endeavour. He counted not the cost. It is, of course, the fate of spirits like that to be disillusioned, repelled, when up against the rough business stuff. They turn away in disgust—do they not?—from the moral compromises, the cunning strategy for mere mercenary gain, of commercial traffic. And so, from this point of view, what more horrible sort of thing could anybody get into than advertising, *alias* "merchandising?"

Our friend was, frankly, hardly prepared for what he found there; was, indeed, even somewhat startled. Astonished, right off the bat, by the body of ethical standards which he discovered had been erected among the leaders in this business. Did he run into a bunch of slick crooks trying to rake in a bale of easy money? A gang in their methods suggesting ambulance-chasing, shyster lawyers? A loud, crash, flashy, over-dressed crew? (That's the way they sound in the books.) Did he run into one of a lot of cut-throat, rival concerns?

His new colleagues were, indeed, more handsomely, and fashionably dressed than, he recalled, he'd usually found journalists to be. They were habitually more pressed, for instance, than either Morley, Don Marquis, or (good heavens!) Heywood Broun. And as to an art director in an advertising agency, it would be nothing less than a shock to come upon one got up in the careless fashion of a first-rate painter

[178]

like, say, George Bellows, or George Luks. If one wanted to be stern, one could say that they, these advertising men, were quite immaculate. Probably, there is point, outside of the traditional arts and the Peerage (I remember in London a figure being pointed out to me, with no little pride, as the worst dressed duke in England), in *looking* successful. But the clothes of our friend's new colleagues were not so audible that you couldn't see their faces. Indeed, the visibility of their garments was not perhaps so high as in the case of, say, A. Edward Newton, nor, certainly not, Joe Hergesheimer. And their faces, mostly more or less youthful, struck him generally as countenances of earnestness and dignity, not infrequently of exceptional character, and, in some cases, even of pronounced distinction.

It was at a convention, early in his advertising experience, that he began to perceive the position that this pursuit had come to occupy in the conception of those who headed it. Far, indeed, from anything like a bumptious air, but gravely, timorously almost, they spoke of it, in various addresses, as a business acquiring the elements of a profession; they who, quietly but obviously, had earnestly at heart its advancement as a calling, and who, it was suddenly apparent to our friend, had been labouring diligently to this end. It was as yet, as an organised activity, a youngster, an infant among the serious affairs of the world. Within the span of hardly more than a score of years it had, from, naturally enough, crude initial stages, made decidedly substantial strides to a consciousness of service responsible to no mean standards. Was it folly to fancy that, perhaps, at some date to come, this modern-born form of human endeavour could approach the status of a career comparable to the ancient walks of medicine and the law?

Suppose one should consider, by way of contrast, the venerableness of the institution of banking, the criterion, perhaps, of business dignity. And yet, here at this convention, the elder advertising men (by a few years) besought their juniors to hold before them in their business contacts the ideals of the banking fraternity. The leading advertising concerns today, to begin with, do not go out after clients with a blackjack; really, they do not perform as barkers for their business, nor act the rôle of pullers-in for second-hand clothing dumps. "Our best prospects are our old clients," as one speaker expressed the matter.

"Think of some of those fine old law firms down town," remarked another. He had in mind the even keel on which they go on generation after generation. Partners pass away but the house continues to stand, four-square. His thought was that an advertising company could, with devotion and character put into it, build in that way, so that in a time to come there might be, too, fine old advertising firms, covered with years and honours. He cherished the hope that the younger men now with his concern would abide there, and continue to carry on the business after he had dropped out, and his partners.

Maybe the analogy is a bit lofty, but let it stand; as universities arrange for the exchange of professors, with the object of expanding their horizon, so now in a similar way do the most progressive advertising houses pool their experience and ambition. Before the assembled staff of a flourishing but comparatively young agency, the other day the dean, perhaps, of the business, and the head of another agency, discussed quite frankly the whys and wherefores of advertising, from the motive, clearly, of inspiring his hearers on to greater accomplishment. He mentioned by the way that probably this was the first time in the history of the business that such an invitation had been extended and accepted; though, indeed, it had now become a matter of repeated occurrence for a member of one firm to sit in counsel on a problem with the members of another firm. All of this, then, you see, and divers other like practices, in the interest of raising the character of the business generally.

Among the first activities of our friend in acquainting himself with the elements of his new business had been an examination of the literature of the "Four A's"—official name, American Association of Advertising Agencies. These reports, it struck him, apparently had never come to the alert attention of any of the numerous humourists, novelists and other lively commentators upon the degradation of the advertising business. . . . Alas! A lot that used to be in this business, our neophyte gathered from these documents, isn't so now. And the thought came over him that the wits and fictionists had evidently got stalled somewhere about five years back in their knowledge of the picture.

Merely a couple of points may serve to illustrate the character of, for one thing, the ethical progress that has been made in the advertising world. The standard of practice today is against the device, held to be obsequious, of an agency's doing any preliminary work on speculation, in the form of a survey, for example, as a bid to a possible client for his business. First rate business and professional services, it is reasoned, should be engaged and not made a gambling matter.

Again, just the other day our excellent humorous weekly, *Life*, had a joke beginning: "ADVERTISING—Reputable New York advertising agency doesn't need a young college graduate, but will give one a good job if he has any influence with any good advertiser;" the fact is that, these days, if a lad comes around looking for a job on the ground of his chance of swinging this or that account along with him he prejudices his case by this method of approach. He is, among those who set the pace, not wanted on that basis—now morally antiquated in the business. The individual equipment of the seeker for employment is made the first consideration; what he may be able to do with his influence, he is to do after he signs up.

[183]

Further, in his own brief observation of the inner works, our friend perceived that repeatedly advertisers who proffered their business were advised, because of this or that to their own advantage, to place it elsewhere. And, now and again, clients who had contemplated an advertising appropriation of something like $40,000 or $50,000 were counselled that it would be more politic for them to spend at the outset perhaps a third as much.

Another thing. He had fancied that the advertising business consisted of advertising, and had supposed that his own particular performance would be to write advertising copy. Somewhat startled, then, he was when early among his duties was put up to him such problems as finding people to fill jobs, at very sizable salaries, with various clients; considering such questions as, "do you know of anyone who would be interested in going into" the manufacture of such-a-thing or other? having tested out at home the merits of some soap, we'll say; sampling table waters; editing books by highly distinguished authors; making speeches before audiences of business librarians, and sundry other congregations; listening to speeches (called "solicitations" or "presentations") on subjects ranging from the "purchasing power" and "buying habits" of followers of the theatre and the history of women's dress patterns to the "retail energy" of grocers and the "small town market;" writing lengthy articles on the (hypothetical) relation of success in movie acting and base-ball infielding to reading the classics of literature; considering the carrying value of various scientifically wrought out juxtapositions of colours; pondering a possible improvement for, maybe, typewriters; seeking an attractive name for a new brand of, well, anything you please, and—and much more.

For, you see, as the matter has developed, nowadays an advertising house of the first rank functions as a business counsellor generally to its clients, and holds about as confidential a relationship to them as, say, a physician to his patients, or the legal adviser to a corporation. An advertising agency may be, behind the scenes, a very considerable constructive power in shaping the policy of a manufacturer, or other clients. It may tell a pants maker (we'll say) that it doesn't altogether like the style of pants he makes, and suggest, perhaps, that he make 'em less fancy. It may invent for him a trick package in which to send out pants to dealers, or something like that. It may take a hand in training his sales force to sell better pants. It may comb the field of "trading centres," gather statistics as to all pants wearers who pay an income tax in the United States, and compose for him a comprehensive chart of pants taste in the Republic. The advertising agency may not only do all this, it may, speaking seriously, do even more; it may influence pants taste in the hinderland, and elevate it to an approach to metropolitan standards.

Even so. I have related the advertising business, in various of its aspects, to the university, the legal calling, and the practice of medicine; I think I'll go right along and take up the pulpit. "The great modern educator is the advertising man," observed Henry Seidel Canby not long ago, in one of his editorials then going in *The Literary Review* of *The New York Evening Post*. "We Americans are the best-informed people in the world. We know a little about everything," he continued, in the course of his remarks concerning "magazine information." As to the "spread of general information" which "makes us more intelligent," he questions, however, whether "it makes us any wiser." Now it might be put forward as, at least, a ponderable idea, whether the printed product of what Dr. Canby respectfully (or, perhaps, ironically) termed the "advertising profession" does not, on the whole, tend to make us *better*.

Flatly, what are the things which day in and day out the bulk of advertising preaches? Are they not these? Thrift, health, success, personal cleanliness, sanitation; the benefits of study, industry, travel; the charm of domestic things, and so on. One might say that, according to Samuel Butler, it preaches the love of God; for was it not his notion that this is to be intelligent, good-looking, well-dressed, and to have a balance in the bank?

Does the advertising man frame up all this stuff with his tongue in his cheek? Some of them, no doubt. A type of advertising man may be found, of lively, practical ability and more than so-so intellectual background, who in person presents an attitude of easy cynicism, and frequently alludes in his conversation to "morons" and "the Babbitts of the country." It might be remarked, by the way, that the use of such bromidiums as these have now become does not altogether prove such a sensitive intelligence, after all. And, also, it may be recorded for whatever it is worth, one of the star advertising copy writers of the country, our friend found, wants to know the first thing about any man, this: How does he stand at home?

Well, well; we've been getting quite intense. Honestly now, isn't a lot of advertising copy absurd and ridiculous stuff? Particularly the sort called "atmosphere advertising?" And is not a considerable amount of advertising now current, even when sensible enough in thought, very poorly written? *Quite* so. And anyone at all sensitive to the quality of writing will find around all the while a good deal of other copy concerning which he could say precisely the same thing, in countless "Sunday stories," many magazine articles, numerous editorial columns, book reviews in various quarters, and in more or less of the most flourishing fiction, even in some of the most prominent of that imported from the soil of John Milton.

To continue. From an old-time comrade of his—a young man for several years a close associate in journalism of Joyce Kilmer, John Bunker, a poet of distinction and a critic of some standing—who some time ago had gone into the advertising business, our friend heard: "I, myself, find advertising—at least my brand of it—more and more entertaining, and I think you will. As a matter of cold fact, I find this work infinitely more stimulating, and even intellectual, than book reviewing for New York newspapers, and other such hack work." The beginnings of his interest in the subject, he said, had sprung from a book on making advertisements, which he named, "a most human and readable affair." Advertising, our friend learned, considering its age has a fairly sizable body of literature excellent in its department. Now when he had been a very young man his thought was to become a painter and illustrator; it was his whole thought; so much did he eat, drink, smoke and sleep with the idea of art that it is doubtful whether he knew who was President. He perceived that there are men like that, as ardent, in the art of advertising; their books, for one thing, show it. A bibliography is appended to this essay.

Hear one who has "always been interested in the subtleties of literary form," the stylist Aldous Huxley. "And now I have discovered the most exciting, the most arduous literary form of all, the most difficult to master, the most pregnant in curious possibilities. I mean the advertisement. . . . Nobody who has not tried to write an advertisement has any idea of the delights and difficulties presented by this form of literature—or shall I say of 'applied literature,' for the sake of those who still believe in the romantic superiority of the pure, the disinterested, over the immediately useful? . . . The problem presented by the Sonnet is child's play compared with the problem of the advertisement. . . . He (the advertisement writer) must persuade them (his audience) to part with their money in a speech that is no longer than many a lyric by Herrick." From "On the Margin."

The writer of first-rate advertising can make about as much use as almost anybody else of a full mind. The hobby of one of the most successful copy writers going, our friend learned, is biography; and this student is reputed to have assembled, in this field, a remarkable library for a young man, under forty. His shelves, marshalling the lives of Napoleon, Lincoln, Franklin, *et al*, are among the prime tools of his trade. An outstanding advertisement, you may have noticed, appeared in the papers not long ago which led off with a quotation from Herodotus. At a recent advertising gathering was read as a sample of style perfectly adapted to its end a passage from (as, with inspirational intention, it was put) the greatest copy writer who ever lived, Shakespeare. In short, at any time something of the best that has been said or thought in the world may serve as a cue for the writer of advertising, well or, indeed, ill, according to the degree of his literacy and taste. Highfalutin' jargon and inept "furrin" phrases, of course, make a sorry spectacle in advertising, just as they are preposterous anywhere else.

Does anybody doubt that the production of advertising presents an opportunity for the play of the alertest kind of news sense? Let's see. Our journalist who had gone into advertising had this to say. A little while ago he had turned through a collection of proofs of advertisements for one department store, and had there come upon haphazard such items as these, among innumerable others of a like kind, which had fed the inspiration of the copy writer: A remark by Rudyard Kipling, concerning "the two sides of a shilling," which he had made on the occasion of his installation as Lord Rector of St. Andrews University; a newspaper human interest story about an old man in Buffalo, past sixty, who had heard so much in praise of Niagara Falls that he intended to risk a forty minute trip out there to see the thing for himself; the announcement of the authorities at Princeton of their estimate of the necessary expense of a four-year course; a *mot* by Frank Tinney in the *American Magazine;* an excerpt from "The Future in America," by H. G. Wells, which called attention to a story by John D. Rockefeller concerning a lesson he had learned in a potato field; a quotation from Edward Bok's autobiography; an account of a novel barbecue in Greene County, Georgia; a word coined by *Collier's Weekly;* the appearance of a certain cartoon by Rollin Kirby, and also one by J. N. Darling; a statement made by Chester B. Van Tassel, publisher of *Asia;* a letter printed in H. I. Phillips's column in the New York *Sun;* a railroad ruling affecting Long Island commuters; the event of an invitation performance of Tony Sarg's Marionettes; a relation by Mrs. Tom Mix in *Photoplay* concerning investing in jewels; a reference to a point made by Joseph H. Choate one time in summing up in court; an observation made by Judge John R. Voorhis on his ninety-fourth birthday; a sob story about a beauty contest at a fancy dress ball on a Pacific liner; an article by F. G. Macomber in *The Nation's Business;* an editorial in the *New York Times;* the title of "Hell Bent fer Heaven;" an allusion to Death Valley Scotty, one time king of spenders along Broadway, in his old age reported broke; anecdote about Massachusetts manufacturer who caught the Fall River boat in a great hurry and landed in New York without luggage; and a recollection by President Coolidge concerning his setting out from Amherst.

This harvest of the world's daily goings on was, most effectively, employed in a highly modern form of advertising, of very engaging elasticity as to copy, called "institutional advertising;" which does not directly and specifically advertise any product of manufacture, but seeks to cultivate good will for a business by making it better and more and more favourably known. And it is a form of advertising in which is now expended, understanding observation will show, an amount of talent and skill quite comparable to that engaged in the best journalism current.

[193]

There would be nothing so inappropriate, our friend cheerfully suggested, in having a Pulitzer Prize for the best advertisement produced during the preceding year, the one considered to most adequately reflect the highest standards of American business, or something like that. In fact, in 1923 a series of eight annual awards for the best newspaper and periodical advertisements in the United States and Canada *was* founded, by Edward W. Bok; the awards, consisting of a gold medal and $8,500 in prizes, being known as the Harvard Advertising Awards, and administered by the Harvard Business School. These awards were offered "in the conviction that advertising, wisely utilised, is a great economic power to broaden markets and decrease the cost of distributing." The donor stipulated that *truth* should be recognised as "the most important factor in practical advertising;" and the juries of award, appointed each year by the Dean of the Harvard Business School from among trained business and professional men, are instructed to lay particular stress on "accuracy and fair statement."

One of the prizes of $1,000 is for the advertisement "most effective in its use of English." And our friend added, that it wouldn't be a bad idea at all for academic courses in English composition to consider, as examples of clean-cut, clear-headed, high-class writing of the day, a selection from among the best specimens of our modern advertising. "I'd say," he declared, "that Stevenson would not scorn to acquaint himself with such samples of lucid, nervous (in the nice meaning of the word), and well-groomed writing."

Probably the mind's eye of the public generally does not pause to see an advertisement *written* at all. Advertisements, people may suppose, just get into magazines and papers along with the real written matter, done by reporters (beings of whom one has heard) and authors (whose portraits may be seen any day). Advertisements are, of course, written in various ways, just as other things—books, for instance,—are written in various ways. We all know (or we all ought to know) that the autobiography of a public man (one distinguished in a field other than literature) frequently is written by a professional writer, who, naturally, for the occasion remains anonymous. Some writers of contemporary literature write, in a wretched-looking dressing-gown, with a soft carbon pencil late at night;

others, smartly attired, dictate in a skyscraper office during the most precise business hours. And so on. Let us then look at, at least, one example of the way in which good advertisements are written, as observed by our friend.

You will have noticed, it is to be hoped, that for some time the blurb has been generally entering less and less into advertising. "Truth in Advertising" was not long ago taken as the keynote of the organised effort of the Associated Advertising Clubs of the World; and one of the most alert and practical books on the business has as a chapter head: "Sincerity—the Most Essential Factor in Copy." More and more we find an advertisement to be a simple statement, made as effective as possible, of the facts in the case, stripped of any other argument. The up-to-scratch advertising man lampoons the "trick words" of the advertising *poseur*.

An amount of work in preparation which may considerably surprise anyone on the outside, often precedes the composition of such a statement. Among the things satirized in the advertising business is the term, regarded as esoteric, *research*. The truth is that all business men have come to a keen realisation that they must have

[196]

facts on which to build and that there must be a systematic searching for these facts. It matters not at all what the process be called, advertising agencies have various names for their fact-finding departments: Statistical Department, Commercial Research, Trade Survey, Bureau of Information, or Library. The work here ranges from the preparation of extensive trade surveys, which may require several months to complete, to such a simple performance as showing a man where in the *World's Almanac* he can find a list of the presidents of the United States. This department is constantly assembling information of value to the house and its customers.

Where our friend got his job the Research Department maintains a staff of seven people, owns a library of more than one thousand volumes, receives regularly over five hundred different magazines and trade papers, keeps up a clipping file of literally thousands of articles, pamphlets, reports and so on; and is called upon to answer, frequently immediately, a dizzy variety of questions. Some :

Have owls ever been used as food? (Answer: Yes, Louis XIV had a *chef* . . .).

How do you say "Red Star" in French, German, Spanish, Japanese, Latin and Greek?
How did the Indian squaw make bread?
Compile a history of underwear.
Give a list of modern slang phrases in use in business.
How many yards of music around a Victrola record?

A great newspaper, to take now a case as a sample, became the client of an advertising agency. The newspaper was as venerable, almost, as the hills; the agency was as young, in a slight figure of speech, as the morning—but that, perhaps, is beside the point. The agency sent down to the newspaper a number of persons to gather data; they interviewed the Editor, the managing editor, financial editor, dramatic editor, society editor, city editor, foreign editor, the sporting editor, and, it is likely, about everybody else of any executive consequence on the paper.

The bacon brought home in the form of research material measured up into something like thirty-five or forty pages, wide measure typing, of compact information. In this was recorded, among much else, such concrete matter as exactly the number of columns and lines of foreign news, of financial news, of sporting news, of society news, and so on, printed by the paper within a recent specified time; the number of news scoops secured by the paper, all within that time, and so on. Then? From all of this was dug out, by a man who had written goodness knows how much for, at one time and another, every important paper in New York City, what may reasonably be assumed to be the points most effective for emphasis in presenting the merits of this paper. This he did not do within the twinkling of an eye. He marshalled a statement for each advertisement, to be one of a short series, in a set of paragraphs of a trifle over a hundred words. And every one of these terse advertisements was entirely rewritten by a colleague, also a former newspaper man. Then the first writer took it upon himself to criticise sundry minor points of style in the work of the second writer, and some of the paragraphs were revised in proof.

Take a look, too, said, in effect, our friend, at this picture: as many as three professional writers of reputable standing and years of experience (all of them, by the way, one time editors of magazines of large national circulation) spending, altogether, hours over the question of one piece of copy—highly paid men, valuable time going by all the while, callers perhaps waiting. Consider, was the tenor of his continuing

remarks, the remarkable case of himself. Here
was one of the most rapidly-growing advertising
houses in the field; would not almost anybody be
likely to think that it would, naturally, say to
itself: "What's the matter with our copy; it's
successful enough, isn't it?" But no, this business concern is *not* satisfied with being merely
successful; it hires no less a personage than himself; and, in heaven's name! what for? . . . In
good measure, to jack-up the copy of the estab-
lishment generally, and bring it nearer to the
pure milk of the written word.

Men of very sizable literary reputation have
put the hand of talent to writing advertising.
Here, perhaps, is a good place to note that
Advertising is not to be (though it very frequently is) confused with what is commonly
called Publicity; a different box of tricks altogether, that—or, more accurately speaking, quite
another art. Advertising fills space which is
bought and paid for, and wears its name openly
upon its face. Publicity cunningly steals its way
into columns popularly supposed to be devoted
to disinterested news. An effectual publicity
man, or "press agent," is a very shrewd and
skilful gamester. The strategic devices of the

wily practitioner of publicity, it is to be re-marked, have in the opinion of numerous leading advertising firms little or no place in the business of straight advertising, and activities in this di-rection desired by clients frequently are dele-gated to other quarters.

As to persons distinguished as writers in other fields who have worked, as a business, at writing *bona fide* advertising copy. Sinclair Lewis was counted, by the publishing house which one time engaged him for a number of years, an exceed-ingly practical writer of advertising for books. Coningsby Dawson preceded him in his job there. Julian Street did brilliant work as a copy writer for the well-known advertising agency of which he was a co-founder. Elbert Hubbard, as everyone knows, wrote a good deal of advertising matter—though, as with everything else he wrote, he did not write it nearly so well as is popularly supposed. That picturesque personal-ity, Gerald Stanley Lee, has, so to put it, done advertising galore. Bruce Barton, whose ex-ceedingly human and stimulating *causeries* have for long been a prized feature of the most widely read magazines, is President of an advertising firm and decidedly active as a copy writer there.

"Not," said our friend (with an emphatic gesture), "that the advertising business is anything of an asylum for the *literati*." Nothing which has been said here has been intended to mean anything other than that the prime function of an advertisement writer is Salesmanship: he is, of course, striving to sell goods by means of printers' ink. "No advertisement," as one man representative of the best in advertising states, "can be successful unless it be a part of a well-thought-out merchandising plan, and unless it is built upon a deep and accurate knowledge of the product, the market, and real or possible competition, and any other factor which affects either the sale or the profit on the sale." And "the true advertising man in his highest and fittest sense," as he is defined by another leader in the business, you face "when in one person you find the Merchant-mind and the Writer-mind working as one."

III

To "tell the story" the advertising business uses pictures more manifold than any other agency concerned with their dissemination.

[202]

ADVERTISING ADVERTISING

Turn through the pages of your magazine and your newspaper and consider something. Comparatively, very few people in the world when they are out walking on Fifth Avenue turn into such places as the Durand-Ruel, Macbeth, Ehrich or Montross galleries, or visit regularly the Metropolitan Museum of Art. But, nevertheless, the daily lives of millions are touched by much of the work of the best painters and graphic artists of our time, most generously through the pages of advertising—truly, "the Art Gallery of Democracy."

Not long ago a man who had written more or less extensively on the subject of art, in fairly authoritative quarters, had an idea that he'd do an article or so (which seemed to be lacking) on contemporary American illustrators, men who might, possibly, be held comparable to the elder masters of the craft, Abbey, Pyle, Gibson, Frost, Yohn, Rinehart, Wenzell, Remington, Arthur Keller and the rest of the gifted and disciplined company who made those golden days of American magazine illustration. He went around to talk it over with Thomas B. Wells, Editor of *Harper's Magazine*, an institution most creditably distinguished for, among other things, the rôle it has played in nurturing American graphic art. "How about the new men of today?" he was asked.

"Why, in the old days," he said, "we used to keep most of those fellows" (he meant the men who established the tradition of excellence in American magazine illustration) "in the back room of our place." In the early eighties there were only a few magazines; two, and then three, leading ones. And, remember, the very limited mechanical processes of reproduction of the time decidedly restricted an artist's powers of expression. In those few magazines, and in the sections of them unrelated to advertising, was practically the sole channel of outlet for illustrative talent. Today, a multiplicity of lavishly illustrated magazines; and it's a sluggish (or a perverse) mind which fails to recognise the bales of advertising pages, gayest of all, as a vast theatre for the exercise, and appreciation, of native art. Innumerable successful, and strikingly able, artists pursue their calling scattered all over the country.

Nobody in his artistic senses will pretend that much advertising illustration is not rotten art; but here we happen to be considering the other side. J. H. Chapin, since 1897 art editor of *Scribner's Magazine*, and whose long service to American magazine illustration has included such brilliant features as the discovery of Walter Appleton Clark, sent the art-article writer, for the most abundant information about the best men of the day, to the art director of an advertising agency. First he showed him, with much gusto, a copy of the quarto-volume, "The Second Annual of Illustrations for Advertisements in the United States" (1923). Mr. Chapin, by the way, was President of the Art Directors Club, 1922-1923.

Now who will dispute that the stream of drawings by a number of men whose names have become synonymous with advertising art, Coles Phillips, Franklin Booth, and others, does not carry to the æsthetically phlegmatic multitude a living interest in the conscientious work of real (if rather minor) talent? The more good art one sees the better is one's taste for it. A roll of the best illustrators here and in England would omit very few who have not contributed abundantly to the educative spectacle, as on the whole it is, of pictorial advertising. At random, one can name: F. R. Gruger, N. C. Wyeth, Dean Cornwell,

Frank Brangwyn, Edmund Dulac, Charles Chambers, Ethel Plummer, Jessie Wilcox Smith, Harvey Dunn, John Held, Hugh Ferris, Willy Pogany, Rea Irvin, Walter Biggs, Douglas Duer, Reginald Birch, William Leftwitch Dodge, Gayle P. Hoskins, William Oberhardt, Pruett Carter, Herbert Paus, S. N. Abbott. And especial mention I should make of a genuinely great artist of our time, a descendant in his craft of Charles Keene, and who has prolifically supplied the daily papers with, literally, masterpieces of spirited draughtsmanship, to advertise a make of men's clothing; I mean Wallace Morgan.

There are men who were established painters of the first rank a long while before they became "advertising men;" the genius of Childe Hassam, just as an instance, has been employed in advertising. There are men whose murals are in the greatest capitols of the world; take Jules Guerin. There are men hung in every gallery; for the matter of that, take the National Academy list and check 'em down; the eye right off lights upon the names of: E. L. Blumenschein, Charles Livingston Bull, Sydney Dickenson, John Newton Howitt. There are the best designers for block-printing, or "wood-cutters:" Rudolph Ruzica, Howard McCormick, J. J. A. Murphy, Will Bradley. There are artists doing advertising work today whose names are as illustrious as these: Timothy Cole and Joseph Pennell. And a fact, perhaps, of peculiar interest is that famous sculptors—among them Paul Manship, Harriet Frismuth, and Charles Hafner—have been commissioned by advertising. Charles Grafley, instructor of Sculpture at the Pennsylvania Academy of Fine Arts, has engaged in work advertising the product of a belting company.

Gesturing toward a reproduction of a still life which had been painted for advertising, said the art director to the art-article writer: "Believe me! in a secession hanging that would win a medal." "It would," said the art-article writer. Thinking now of advertising as a *patron* of art—and, because a very wealthy, a powerful one—there is as "food for thought" this doubtless little known circumstance; advertising agencies, sometimes, employ young men with a nose for talent to act as "scouts," whose business it is to find the most promising unrecognised talent and to operate in nursing it along. As a cultural influence in the

nation the advertising business acts in a direct
and practical way in this: the advertising agency
must "sell" the "art" it has produced for an advertisement to the advertiser; in other words, it
is often necessary for an agency to educate the
taste of a manufacturer or merchant to the point
of appreciating the work of the artist it would
have him buy. And it's as true as anything you
know, that a very much larger amount of good
art would be presented in advertising if it could
be put across on the minds of the advertisers.
An imposing display of what is being done in
this field is exhibited each Spring in the Annual
Exhibition of Advertising Art, held at Art
Centre, New York City.

Come now, what makes the advertising business so keen as all this about Art? The advertising director of an important national manufacturer recently said:

I have found, by actual test, again and again, that
Beauty is the force by which greater results are easiest
gained and maintained. . . . If an advertisement does not
instantly suggest, even to the man who reads as he runs,
the worth of the product, it does a slip-shod job feebly and
expensively.

So. The best typographers in the world find

in advertising, not only their most generous re-
ward, but their greatest opportunity for expression. A very small number of people, naturally,
bought not long ago, when the work was published, "Printing Types: Their History, Forms,
and Use," by D. B. Updike, two octavo volumes,
Harvard University Press, $15.00 a set—a mon-
ument in its field. The world in general imbibes
all it knows of the rich art of typography mainly
from the daily and the periodical press; and,
when you think of it, in these organs the only
display of typographical versatility is in the advertising columns.

The type which Horace Greeley used before
the Civil War, and the type in which the Keeley
Cure advertisements were set up, are now pretty
much obsolete everywhere. We set most of our
advertisements and our good magazines today in
type faces which have honourable histories, and
were designed by first-rate artists working after
unassailable ancient models. Will Bradley bids
typographers to "Tickle your type and make it
smile." From the type employed in an advertisement the reader may judge the quality of the
message of the text and whether it would prove

interesting to him—it may contribute to his pleasure in looking at a page without his ever being conscious of the cause.

People frequently say of a book that it *looks* like good reading. The object behind the use of classic type in an advertisement is to make it think, and talk, and get action. Great store is set by the alert modern advertising man on the physical appearance of an advertisement. One prominent advertising director states: "The deeper my experience goes the more importance I place upon *form* and the less upon *matter*. What is said in an advertisement is not of first importance. What is suggested is the paramount consideration."

To this end, labour in the vineyard of advertising the most devout students of Theodore De Vinne, and such modern master craftsmen as Frederick Goudy, T. M. Cleland, Bruce Rogers, and W. A. Dwiggins; among a younger generation of erudite typographers men like Everett Currier, W. Arthur Cole, Fred Singleton, David Silve, David Gildea, and the late Benjamin Sherbow, who developed the "Sherbow Type Charts for Advertising," which bring the classical standards to the layman. Striven for, through Beauty, is the realisation of what Herbert Spencer called the principle of the Economy of Attention, the principle of variety, and the principle of *fitness*. The Manager of Art and Mechanical Production Departments at the advertising agency which engaged the services of our old journalist friend harps continually upon "using the old masters as our guide," Tory, Garamond, Baskerville, Caslon, and Bodoni. "I can think right now," he observed one day, "of a series of simple merchandise advertisements that might be done after Geoffery Tory, by a contemporary master designer like Teague or Rogers, that would at once be so beautiful and so effective in the matter of display that the individual pieces *could not* be missed by any eye roving over a modern newspaper page."

How do ya' get Good Taste?. . . . In a sensitivity to typography, or anything else? Well, as Royal Cortissoz, dean of American art critics, puts the matter, you get it by "a constant interrogation" of the enduring achievements of the past. And that roving eye of the great public, albeit indirectly and unconsciously, does this very thing by continually looking at the typography of the profuse advertising matter of today. Also, a good deal could be said about another matter, but there is time for very little concerning it here. You probably get in the course of your mail a good many circulars, cards, pamphlets and so on, advertising this and that. In a brief address to his associates in the business, "Ten Minutes with the Practical Side," recently an art director opened thus: "To get good final printing results: Start Right! *Think first of paper*—the medium upon which the message is to be conveyed." Now Paper may not consciously mean much to you, but with some men it is a passion: the romance of its history, the varieties of its beauty, and the application of its fitness to a given end. To most people, the only education vouchsafed them in the nuances of paper is supplied by the advertising matter which comes to them by post. And, further, among the things you see at the store—boxes of soap, sometimes, or crackers—there is, speaking quite seriously, something in the way of culture to be got. Cartons and containers have been designed by Tommy Cleland, for one, which are art, as much as any trinket fashioned by Benvenuto Cellini.

[212]

IV

The letter of invitation read much like this: *We should be very glad indeed to have you talk to us on the business of writing. Our Club is a group of practical writers in various fields, who would welcome the opportunity to hear your views on such a subject.* Our journalist friend had (out of his experience) written a good deal, and talked more or less, on various phases of the business of writing: marketing magazine and newspaper articles and stories, publishing plays, the field of book reviewing, the work of the publicity man, and so on. He had heretofore said little about advertising because of his lack of acquaintance with the matter. Now, however, he felt that he had something to communicate in regard to this department of the business of writing, which should be of interest, and might be of some service, to "a group of practical writers in various fields."

One lady present insisted, just before the program of the meeting, upon his trying one of her favourite brand of cigarettes, and a gentleman engaged him in conversation upon the subject of Whitman. He asked our friend if he did not

consider Whitman "our greatest poet." Soon
they were going to have a Whitman meeting.
Our friend was ardently beamed upon by the
audience as he was formally introduced, in a
speech which abounded in caressing allusions to
Montaigne, Addison, Steele, Lamb—and himself.

His talk consisted, in substance, of about what
has been said here. Very shortly after he had got
under way it was patent that he was not being
found the delightful fellow that had been expected. Several of his audience walked out on
him cold. There was, more or less roundabout,
something like a hostile glint in the eye of the
rest. Evidently, he was *not* saying what they
wanted to hear. When he sat down, it was soon
quite plain that, actually, he had thrown a bomb
into this gathering, which outraged all that its
members held sacred.

Instantaneously, in response to an invitation
from the chairman for any "comment," a very
vigorous lady arose and declared that the first
thing she did with any advertisement was to "tear
it out and throw it away." (Loud applause.)
She said several minutes more to a similar effect,
all of which received hearty audible approbation.

A person then got up, who it appeared was present as a guest, and broke out real vitriolic. He declared that the great trouble with this country (it was not his country, by the way; he was a Scot) was the "herd" habit, and that the most pernicious corrupter of civilisation was advertising; but some brand or other of "chewing gum" could not by advertising be "rammed down" *his* throat. With scathing irony he "excused" the advertising man his iniquity, because what he did was done for *money*. The impassioned speaker spoke the word "money" a good many times, and each time it was as though he had said "viper."

But his greatest unction was exercised when, in reference to the writer of advertising, he spoke (to a general nodding of heads in acquiescence) that terrible word "prostitute." It appeared in the course of his remarks that this person's business was running a newspaper syndicate— whether or not he ran it for "money," who can say? But he called high heaven to witness that he had never sought to further his business by one single line of advertising. A critical listener might have thought it a bit odd that the fact seemed never to occur to him that without advertising there would be no newspapers, and conse-

[215]

quently no newspaper syndicates; that is, a newspaper would be able to appear only about once a month, and a copy of it would cost the reader as much as a portly book. One of the most popular weekly magazines costs forty-seven cents a copy to manufacture, sells wholesale at three cents, and to the reading public at five cents. Its famous and highly paid authors and artists are living on advertising.

A few faint voices spoke up in defence of our unfortunate friend; it was meekly suggested that things other than chewing gum might be advertised; that, for instance, an advertisement might remind one to make one's will, and protect one's estate; that bread, say, could be advertised—no "creation of a new want;" and that advertising rendered the public service of carrying the news as to how much things are. Much more might have been said, by one familiar with the matter, concerning the diversity of the uses of advertising. Advertising, forsooth, has been employed to meet unfavourable legislation, enforce court decrees, draw the fangs from evil gossip, develop a new business street, help place inexperienced men on farms, protect expiring copyrights, overcome prejudice against department store employment, halt a crime wave, keep people out of lawless taxicabs, put health on the map, prevent suicide, sell buried treasure, and make the telephone user forswear profanity. Many illuminating articles on the widely various uses of advertising have appeared in *Printers' Ink,* the most comprehensive of these, "Advertising— And Its Unusual Uses," in *Printers' Ink Monthly,* September, 1922.

But there could be no doubt of the controlling sense of that meeting: advertising, to say the least, was unnecessary; and our poor friend was a woeful spectacle of a soul that had capitulated. The things which high minds hankered for were the Good, the Pure, and the Beautiful. The meeting broke up somewhat in disorder.

Our friend's head was bloody but unbowed. He has the hardihood still to contend that people of this kind are pretending to be superior to something which they are not, as *artists,* capable of doing well. That *their's* is the Bunkum.

Selected Bibliography

Founded on the basic books on advertising as selected by leading men in that field for inclusion in the business library of the McAlpin Hotel, and announced by L. M. Boomer, December, 1923.

LITERARY LANES

A Short Course in Advertising. By Alex F. Osborn (Scribner, 1921).

Making Advertisements and Making Them Pay. By Roy S. Durstine (Scribner, 1920).

Principles of Advertising. By Daniel Starch, Ph.D., Graduate School of Business Administration, Harvard University (A. W. Shaw Company, 1923).

The Advertising Handbook: A Reference Work Covering the Principles and Practice of Advertising. By S. Roland Hall (McGraw-Hill Book Company, Inc., 1921).

Advertising as a Business Force. By Paul T. Cherington (Doubleday, 1913).

Imagination in Business. By L. F. Deland (Atlantic Monthly, 1909, Boston).

The Theory of Advertising. By Walter Dill Scott (Small Maynard, 1903, Boston).

Human Nature in Selling Goods. By J. R. Collins (H. Altemus Co., 1909, Philadelphia).

Selling Forces. By Richard J. Walsh (Curtis Publishing Company, 1913).

Making Type Work. By Benjamin Sherbow (Century, 1919).

Effective Type-Use for Advertising. By Benjamin Sherbow (B. Sherbow, 1922).

Marketing Problems. By M. T. Copeland (A. W. Shaw Company, 1920).

Trade Mark Power. By Glen Buck (Munroe & Southworth, 1916, Chicago).

Advertising, Its Principles and Practice. By Harry Tipper, George Burton Hotchkiss, Harry L. Hollingworth and Frank Alvah Parsons (Ronald Press, 1915).

The Art Appeal in Display Advertising. By Frank Alvah Parsons (Harper, 1921).

The Business of Advertising. By Ernest Elmo Calkins (Appleton, 1920).

Typography of Advertisements That Pay. By Gilbert P. Farrar (Appleton, 1917).

[218]

ADVERTISING ADVERTISING

ESSENTIALS OF ADVERTISING. By Frank Leroy Blanchard (McGraw-Hill, 1921).

ADVERTISING COPY. By George Burton Hotchkiss, M.A., Chairman, Department of Advertising and Marketing, New York University; President, National Association of Teachers of Advertising (Harper, 1924).

ADVERTISING AND SELLING. By H. L. Hollingworth (Appleton, 1920).

ADVERTISING FOR THE RETAILER. By Lloyd D. Herrold. (Appleton).